The Beckwith Dynasty
A Ranching Empire in Colorado's Wet Mountain Valley

The Beckwith Dynasty

A Ranching Empire in Colorado's Wet Mountain Valley

Courtney Miller

Filter Press, LLC

The Beckwith Dynasty: A Ranching Empire in Colorado's Wet Mountain Valley
Copyright © 2024 by Courtney Miller
First edition

Published by Filter Press, LLC

ISBN: (Paperback): 978-0-86541-263-7

Library of Congress Control Number: 2024935779

Cover design: Jordan Ellender
Cover photograph: Filter Press

Filter Press, LLC
Westcliffe, Colorado
https://www.filterpressbooks.com/

To the volunteers, past and present, who helped restore the Beckwith Ranch and have kept it alive

Contents

List of Figures

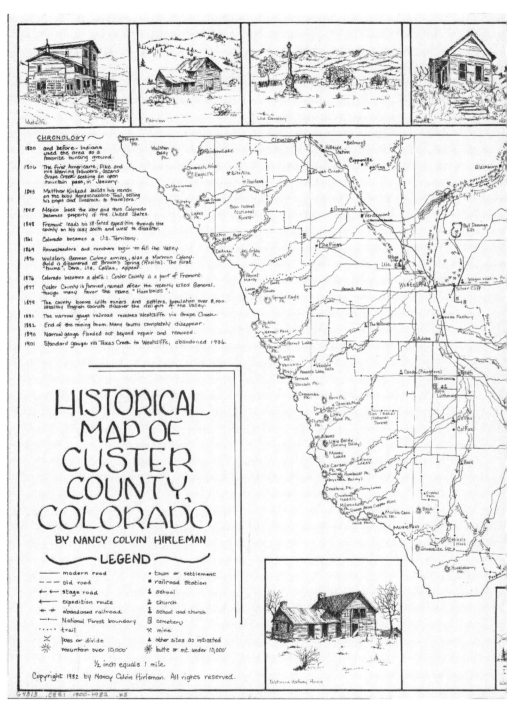

Historical map of Custer County drawn by
Nancy Colvin Hirleman, 1982

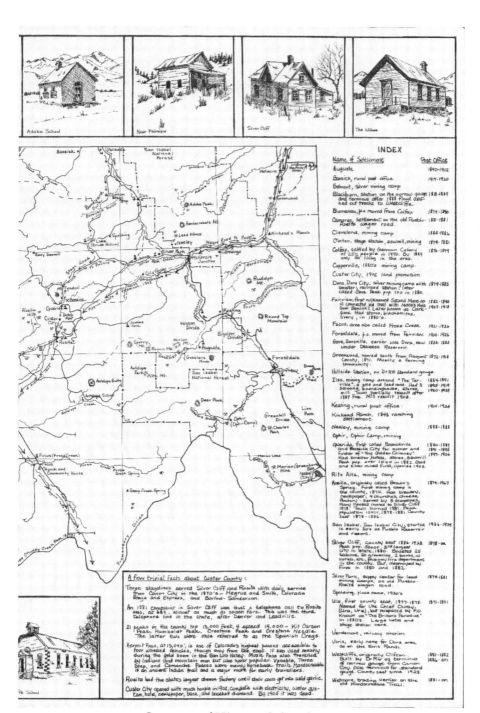

INDEX

A few trivial facts about Custer County:

Three stagelines served Silver Cliff and Rosita with daily service from Canon City in the 1870's – Hegrue and Smith, Colorado Stage and Express, and Barlow-Sanderson.

An 1881 complaint in Silver Cliff was that a telephone call to Rosita was, at 55¢, almost as much as coach fare. This was the third telephone line in the state, after Denver and Leadville.

21 peaks in the county top 13,000 feet, 4 exceed 14,000 – Kit Carson Peak, Humboldt Peak, Crestone Peak and Crestone Needle. The latter two were once referred to as the Spanish Crags.

Hermit Pass, at 13,040', is one of Colorado's highest passes accessible to four wheeled vehicles, though only from the east. It was used mostly during the gold boom in the San Luis Valley. Music Pass also travelled by Indians and mountain men but was never popular. Venable, Three Step, and Comanche Passes were mainly horseback trails. Hardscrabble is an ancient Indian trail and a major route for early travellers.

Rosita had the state's largest cheese factory until their cows got into wild garlic.

Custer City opened with much hoopla in 1902, complete with electricity, water system, hotel, newspaper, bank, and baseball diamond. By 1905 it was dead.

Adobe School

Near Fairview

Silver Cliff

The Willows

__ School

Figure 1: The Beckwith Ranch, 2024
Courtesy of the Matt Richter Collection

CHAPTER 1

The Patriarch: George Chipman Beckwith

The Wet Mountain Valley in south-central Colorado is a remote and rural community whose past is still very evident. Two small towns, Silver Cliff and Westcliffe, butt up against each other in the center of the valley—unpretentious, quiet, and friendly.

Just north of Westcliffe, on Highway 69, ten buildings with white clapboard siding and bright red roofs sit west of the highway. You can't miss them. Their unique Victorian style grabs your attention as they glisten quietly and contrast so greatly with the traditional ranching pastures and homes that surround them.

The main mansion, with its unique *porte cochère* (carriage porch) reaching out from the front door, begs the question, "What happened here?"

Many curious travelers pull into the dirt driveway and park in front of two small cottages sitting just south of the glorious old mansion. Most visitors first stop at a large interpretive sign to quench their curiosity about the unique structures.

Next they are compelled to take photographs of the two little cottages beside the two-story mansion before crossing over to the mansion, and then on to the bunkhouse, tack barn, and workshop. The horse barn and dairy barns, whose cupulas sport impressive weathervanes featuring racehorses, are viewed last. The magnificent Sangre de Cristo Mountains rise up west of the buildings to produce a postcard-ready photograph.

The impeccably restored buildings were once the headquarters of one of Colorado's largest and most successful cattle ranches, referred to today simply as the Historic Beckwith Ranch. It is one the most photographed sites in Colorado.

This is the story of the Beckwiths, the men and women who built and operated the ranch from 1869 to 1907. George Beckwith and his sons Elton and Edwin along with Elton's

**Figure 2: The old Beckwith barn with a cupula
sporting a weathervane of a racehorse**
Courtesy of the Charlie Whyte collection

Figure 3: George Chipman Beckwith, circa 1880
Courtesy of the Holly Davis Collection

wife, Elsie, and their daughter, Velma, possessed extraordinary vision and drive. The typical settler of this period came to the Wild West and adapted to it. The Beckwiths came west expecting that their new home would adapt itself to them.

The Beckwiths' story begins in Nova Scotia, Canada, with the birth of George Chipman Beckwith on July 24, 1817. He was the ninth of ten children born to Holmes Marvin Beckwith and Eunice Ann Pineo.

Marvin Beckwith was born and died in Halifax, Nova Scotia, which was a center for shipbuilding at the time. Marvin's parents, Samuel Beckwith and Rebecca Chapman, had moved to Halifax from Norwich, Connecticut, after the Revolutionary War. Marvin married Eunice Ann Pineo on March 12, 1797, and they had ten children. When George Chipman Beckwith was born, Marvin was forty-eight and

Eunice was forty-one.

George grew up working in the shipbuilding industry, where he learned the trade. He was an independent and resourceful man and proved to be an exceptional businessman.

Halifax's shipbuilding industry began in 1751 when the governor offered ten shillings per ton for every new vessel produced.

In 1835, at age eighteen, George moved to New York City, where he worked and saved for nine years. Then he traveled to Boston, Massachusetts, where he became a naturalized citizen of the United States on April 15, 1844, at age twenty-seven. In his naturalization papers, George states that he is a resident of Eden, Maine. In 1900 Eden became the town of Bar Harbor on Mount Desert Island. It was in Eden where George started his own shipbuilding business, married, and began his family.

According to an article in the May 6, 1965, *Bar Harbor Times*, shipbuilding and sailing were important business enterprises for the small community. The article begins by quoting Eben Hamor's unpublished history of Bar Harbor:

> "The most profitable and perhaps the most extensive business engaged in by the early settlers of Eden was building vessels and sailing them. . . ." [Hamor] states that 106 vessels were built in Eden from 1809 to 1860. . . . Among his listings of them are: . . .
>
> Schr. W. P., 128 tons, William Peach, master, Eben L. Higgins, James Hamer, Samuel H. Richards (all Eden), Nathan King and Isaac Hodgkins, Trenton, John Jordan, Ellsworth, George C. Beckwith, Mount Desert, owners.

Barren, treeless, and rocky, Mount Desert Island rises from the ocean off the central coast of Maine like a giant turtle. The name Mount Desert (pronounced like dessert or deserted) Island fits it perfectly. The winters are cold and snowy, and summers are short and mild, averaging around seventy degrees. Mount Desert Island is only 370 miles south of Halifax, Nova Scotia, where George was born and raised.

It was on Mount Desert Island where George met his bride, Tamesin Heath, a local girl. The two married and raised five children: three boys and two girls. Loring Everett was born on February 12, 1845; Elton Towers on April 1, 1847; Edwin F. on April 4, 1849; Velma (sometimes spelled Vellma) in 1854; and Idella in 1856.

With the gold rush starting in California in 1848, it was a good time to get into ship building. The 1850 US Census shows George and his family living in Ellsworth, Maine. On July 17, 1857, an article in a local newspaper, the *Ellsworth American*, describes the launching of George's schooner, the *Quindaro*.

The US Civil War, from 1861 to 1865, furthered George's fortune in shipbuilding and his merchant marine business. George found it was very lucrative to help the Union in the

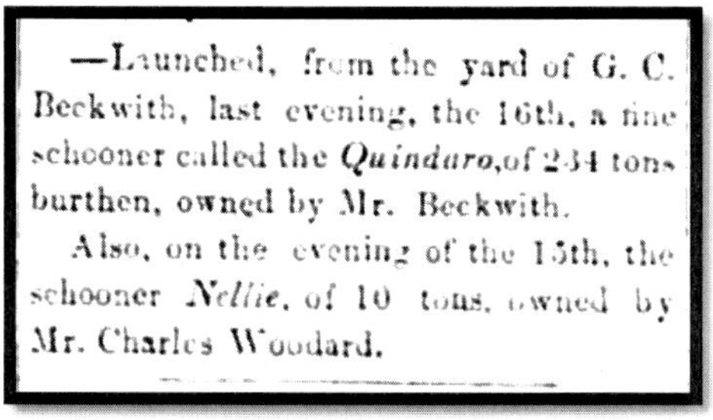

—Launched, from the yard of G. C. Beckwith, last evening, the 16th, a fine schooner called the *Quindaro*, of 234 tons burthen, owned by Mr. Beckwith.

Also, on the evening of the 15th, the schooner *Nellie*, of 10 tons, owned by Mr. Charles Woodard.

Figure 4: The *Ellsworth American*, July 17, 1857, describing the launch of George's Schooner, the *Quindaro*

war. One ship could earn $750,000 (around $26 million today) hauling freight and troops and assisting in Union blockades against the Confederacy.

But, as time would tell, George Beckwith would put his children and their success above all else.

Figure 5: Mount Desert Island, Maine, 1881

Courtesy of Hancock County Atlas, Maine State Archives, 29069,
digitalmaine.com

CHAPTER 2

The Brothers

When their first child Loring Everett Beckwith was born, George was twenty-eight and Tamesin twenty-two. Loring was considered the intellectual of the family and attended Harvard during the Civil War instead of serving on one of George's merchant marine vessels. He hoped to become an Episcopalian minister.

The other two sons, Elton Towers and Edwin F., worked in their father's shipyard until age twelve. Then they transferred to their father's merchant marine business, which sailed up and down the East Coast of the United States transporting goods. According to a short biography in the *History of the Arkansas Valley, Colorado* published in 1881, Elton was "on the sea for four years, three of which he was First Mate of the vessel." Elton had proved himself a capable and trusted seaman. As first mate, he was second in command of the vessel.

Figure 6: Portrait and signature of Elton Beckwith published in the *History of the Arkansas Valley, Colorado,* **1881**

Elton was a handsome, popular, outgoing youth. He was born and raised in an environment of wealth and hard work and was taught to be self-reliant, confident, and independent. Edwin was more reserved and quieter but would prove to be very capable and ambitious.

The blockade by the North against the Confederacy changed the balance of power in the Civil War by cutting off imports of war material, medical supplies, and household goods. It also prevented the sale of cotton abroad by the Confederacy.

In 1863, when Elton turned sixteen, his service in the Civil

War ended. The 1860 US census records George and his family living in Cambridge, Massachusetts, where George's oldest son, Loring, was attending Harvard College.

Instead of following in Loring's footsteps, Elton attended Comer's Commercial College in Boston. Comer's was a private college in a large, square, three-story building at 323 Washington Street. A large sign stating, "Comer's Commercial College" covered most of the second floor.

Comer's Commercial College was no Harvard, but there was probably no better college for an education in nautical studies, engineering, and drafting. Having his son attend Comer's suggests that George had plans for Elton to join him in his shipbuilding and merchant marine businesses after graduation. It is likely he hoped Elton would one day take over the family business.

Elton may not have been interested in attending Harvard, but he later revealed, when he established his own business, that he did not want to follow in his father's footsteps with a career in shipbuilding and the merchant marines.

Comer's Commercial College advertised itself as:

the only establishment for practical instruction in PENMANSHIP, BOOK KEEPING, NAVIGATION, ENGINEERING, which has continued in uninterrupted and successful operation in Boston during the past sixteen years with upwards of SEVEN THOUSAND STUDENTS having attended [and] has thereby peculiar facilities for providing suitable Employment for its graduates who are distinguished in the Naval, Merchant, Military, and Civil Service throughout the world.

Given Comer's focus, Elton would have had no doubt why his father had enrolled him there. His father was a second-

**Figure 7: An advertisement for Comer's Commercial
College from the August 1, 1857, *Boston Pilot***

generation shipbuilder, and it was probably just assumed that
one of his sons would carry on the tradition.

Elton was a good student at Comer's and graduated after
two years in 1865. Edwin enrolled in Comer's the year after
Elton graduated. Elton's dream of independence was realized
when his education and the contacts he made at the college,
along with the financial assistance of his father, helped him to
set up a flour and grain business in Philadelphia,
Pennsylvania. By 1867, Elton was listed as owning a Flour,
Feed & Grain business in McElroy's and Co's Philadelphia
City Business Directory.

Although his father was most likely disappointed that

Elton had chosen not to follow in his footsteps, George would continue to be financially involved in Elton's businesses throughout his life. And although none of George's children followed him into the shipbuilding business, he supported all of his children in their endeavors.

Elton's flour and grain business provided him with some independence and enabled him to hone his business acumen, but Elton faced stiff competition from the dozens of other flour and grain businesses operating in Philadelphia. Therefore, the business would not prove to be as lucrative as his father's shipbuilding business and probably left Elton wanting more.

Edwin graduated from Comer's Commercial College two years after Elton did and would seek his fortune away from his father's shipbuilding business as well.

CHAPTER 3

The Beckwith Women

The matriarch of the family, Tamesin Heath, was of English decent, a native of Mount Desert Island, Maine, and a descendant of the Revolutionary War hero, General William Heath. She was born March 9, 1823, and she married George Chipman Beckwith in 1844 on Mount Desert Island. By 1869, her failing health was one of the reasons George Beckwith decided to move his family to Denver. Colorado was noted for its healthy climate, but it did not prevent her passing away four years later, in 1873. Her untimely death at age fifty precluded her from being involved in the Beckwith ranching dynasty.

Just as the Beckwith men brought strength and business sense to Colorado and the Wet Mountain Valley, Elsie A. Chapin Davis, who married Elton Beckwith in 1875, brought her own strength, culture, and vision. She became known simply as Mrs. Beckwith to the residents of the valley.

Elsie A. Chapin was born on December 6, 1845, in

Figure 8: Elsie Beckwith, circa 1900
Courtesy of the Old Westcliffe Schoolhouse Collection
Photo by Eugenia Ransom Kennicott

Cincinnati, Ohio, the daughter of Polly Rockwell Stone and Oliver Adams Chapin. Oliver was a wealthy and successful shoe manufacturer. Elsie grew up accustomed to the finer things, graduating from Michigan Female Academy in Detroit and attending college at Ogontz School for Young Ladies in Philadelphia.

Elsie married Charles Davis on September 7, 1871. Charles was born in Portland, Oregon, in 1845, and according to the US census he was living with or visiting his brother Joseph Davis in Ula, Colorado, in 1870. Elsie and Charles settled in the Wet Mountain Valley and established the Half Circle D Ranch near Ula. Charles had contracted tuberculosis and hoped the Wet Mountain Valley climate would help him recover, but he passed away in 1873. Elsie took over the ranch after his passing and continued to operate the ranch for many years. In 1874, Elton Beckwith, whose ranch was located near the Half Circle D Ranch, began courting Elsie.

Elsie was an Episcopalian, and according to her obituary in the August 18, 1931, *Rocky Mountain News*, she "was active in work of St. John's Cathedral until her death." A great account about Elsie written by Bet Kettle, a descendant of valley settler Will Kettle, states, "Mrs. Beckwith lacked her husband's easy charm and never took well to the country life and plain people of the valley. She was, in fact, something of a snob and few were comfortable in her fine home, if invited at all."

Elton and Elsie had only one child, a daughter, Elsie Velma. She was named after her mother and Elton's sister. Her exact birthday is uncertain since her mother tended to fib about their ages on census reports and a birth certificate has not been found. Based on US census reports, her birth date could have been in 1876, 1878, 1879, or 1882. Her death certificate states she was fifty years old at the time of her death, which would put her birth in 1881. Other records show that she was fifty-two years old at death, putting her birth in 1879. Perhaps the most reliable source for her birthdate is the biography of her father in the *History of the Arkansas Valley*, Colorado, published in 1881. It states Elton "has one child, a daughter, four years old," which places Velma's birth in 1876-1877.

Velma was the future of the Beckwith dynasty, and by all accounts her family dotted on her. It appears that as a young girl, Velma was headstrong, healthy, and a typical cowgirl, loving to hang around her uncle Edwin on the ranch. She attended college at Ogontz School for Young Ladies in Philadelphia, following the pattern of her parents as a privileged, well-educated young lady.

Elsie's mother, Polly Rockwell Stone Chapin, was born on December 7, 1816, in Providence, Rhode Island. She married

Figure 9: Elsie Velma Beckwith (assumed), sitting, circa 1900.

Courtesy of History Colorado, Accession #98.273.28
Photo by Eugenia Ransom Kennicott

Oliver Adams Chapin on April 25, 1842, in Milford, Massachusetts. They had three boys and two girls. Elsie was the oldest girl with one older brother. Oliver passed away sometime between 1860 and 1870, and Polly moved to the valley to be with her daughter. She also brought her sons, and they homesteaded land and worked for Elton.

CHAPTER 4

The Wet Mountain Valley

While Elton was working to make his flour and grain business successful, Edwin graduated from Comer's Commercial College. It appears that after graduation, Edwin began looking west. In 1865, Horace Greeley wrote an editorial for the *New York Tribune* and made the phrase "Go West, young man, and grow up with the country" popular. This, along with excitement about the Pikes Peak gold rush, may well have influenced Edwin's decision to go west to what was then the Colorado Territory.

The concept of westward expansion took root in 1803 when President Thomas Jefferson purchased the Louisiana Territory. This huge increase in US land led to the concept of Manifest Destiny. This cultural belief drove many settlers west on a mission to expand the US dominion and to spread democracy, capitalism, and the special virtues of the agrarian culture across the entire North American continent. It was a form of "romantic nationalism" by which the nation derived political legitimacy for expanding its language, race, ethnicity, culture, religion, and customs beyond its borders as a moral providence.

But perhaps more importantly to Edwin, the West offered an opportunity to escape the oppressive urban sprawl and industrialization of the eastern United States. It offered a return to the agricultural way of life that the Europeans had brought to the New World. It also offered a chance to escape the factories and complexities that the Industrial Revolution was bringing to American culture.

We may never pinpoint why Edwin and his father decided to go to Colorado in 1869, but among the many reasons, it is clear that they went to Colorado to explore homesteading in the Wet Mountain Valley. For their service, Union veterans of the Civil War qualified for special exemptions under the Homestead Act of 1862, which granted citizens up to 160 acres of public land provided they established a permanent residency on the land for five years, built a home on it, and made improvements. Union veterans could deduct the time they had served in the Civil War from the five-year residency requirement. In addition, Civil War veterans could receive a land grant for an additional 160 acres of land.

In 1869, there was no train service in Colorado. Colorado was truly the Wild West at that time. But it was possible to get to Colorado by taking the train to Cheyenne, Wyoming, and then the stagecoach to Denver. The *Rocky Mountain News* reported stagecoach arrivals and departures, and these records show that Edwin first traveled alone to the Colorado Territory, arriving in Denver on June 15, 1869. What he was doing during this visit is uncertain, and no record has been found to prove that he traveled to the Wet Mountain Valley. Still he must have been impressed with the land and opportunities he found because he returned via stagecoach to Cheyenne on

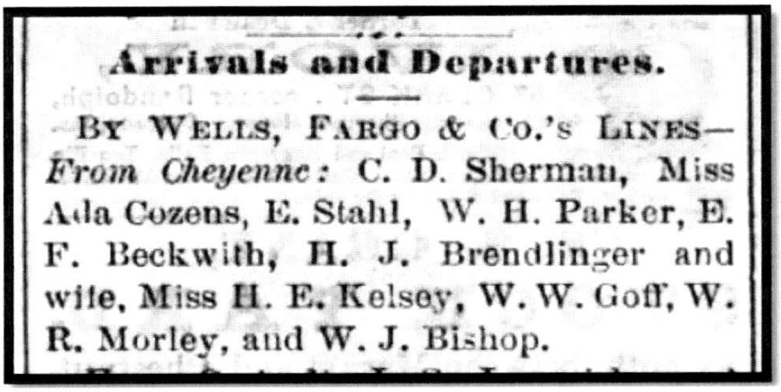

Arrivals and Departures.

BY WELLS, FARGO & CO.'S LINES—*From Cheyenne:* C. D. Sherman, Miss Ada Cozens, E. Stahl, W. H. Parker, E. F. Beckwith, H. J. Brendlinger and wife, Miss H. E. Kelsey, W. W. Goff, W. R. Morley, and W. J. Bishop.

Figure 10: Stagecoach arrival from Cheyenne, including Edwin (E. F.) Beckwith, reported in the *Rocky Mountain News* on June 15, 1869

August 3, 1969, and on his next visit just two months later, he was accompanied by his father, George Beckwith.

Edwin and George boarded the John Hughes & Co. stage line, arriving in Denver on October 15, 1869. They spent the next several weeks exploring the area and traveling by stagecoach to Georgetown and Central City and back to Denver. On November 3, 1869, the *Rocky Mountain News* reported that they took a stagecoach "To the South." This most likely means George and Edwin took Abraham Jacobs' Denver & Santa Fe Stage from Denver to Pueblo. When George returned alone to Denver on December 10, 1869, the *Rocky Mountain News* listed him as traveling "Per A. Jacobs' Line."

Once in Pueblo, they could have purchased horses or mules, tack, and supplies and ridden west toward the Wet Mountains across Charles Goodnight's Rock Canyon Ranch. After the civil war, Charles Goodnight and his friend Oliver Loving rounded up longhorn cattle ranging free across Texas and drove them north to sell. The trail they established became known as the Goodnight-Loving Trail. In 1868, Goodnight purchased around sixteen thousand acres of land to graze his Texas longhorn cattle in Colorado. At that time, Goodnight was already famous as a Texas Ranger, Indian fighter, and Civil War scout.

The Rock Canyon Ranch was huge. It stretched west of Pueblo and followed the Arkansas River on its northwest side to the base of the Wet Mountains, where Florence is today. On the south, it stretched almost to the current-day town of Beulah. The ranch was one-third of the Gervacio Nolan Spanish land grant. At that time, Goodnight was making a good living selling the longhorns from Texas to local homesteaders and ranchers in Colorado. It is likely that George and Edwin met with Goodnight, if for no other reason than to ask permission to cross his ranch to get to the Wet Mountain Valley.

After a long day's ride from Pueblo, Edwin and George might have made camp at the base of the Wet Mountains at Goodnight's Babcock's Hole line camp near the present-day town of Wetmore. At that time, the best way to cross the Wet Mountains to reach the Wet Mountain Valley was to follow

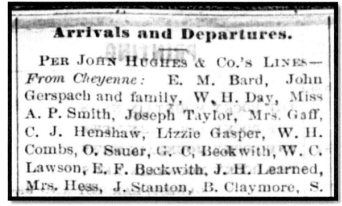

Figure 11: Stagecoach arrival from Cheyenne, including Edwin (E. F.) Beckwith and his father, George (G. C.) Beckwith, reported in the *Rocky Mountain News* on October 25, 1869

the creek that flowed down Hardscrabble Canyon. The path up Hardscrabble Canyon was rocky, steep, and narrow, and would have required them to walk and lead their horses as much as ride.

On November 13, 1872, the *Colorado Daily Chieftain* published a delightful article detailing the trail over the southern portion of the Wet Mountains (called the Greenhorns at that time). This account was written only three years after Edwin and George may have traversed it:

> Having finished our business on Hardscrabble, we set out on the morning of a beautiful sunshiny day, for the ride across Greenhorn Mountains through Hardscrabble Pass. This road is the same towards the construction of which, Pueblo-ites contributed fifteen hundred dollars; it leads into a deep dark canon, in which is a dense growth of scrub oak, pinon, and small cottonwoods, many of which are completely covered with the beautiful wild clematis vine, with its showy snow-white plumes, and the effect is very fine, heightened as it is, by the great loftly jagged walls of rock on either side. Here the admirer of the grand sublimities of nature can gaze with satisfaction, and exclaim with unfeigned feeling, "how wonderful are thy works, O Lord." But the teamster traveling through with a load, would, we fear, indulge in such outbursts of profanity, as would almost cause the ponderous rocks to fall on him and send him into eternity unshriven. Such a wagon road intended for public travel we never saw before; although it is not a steep grade, it is nevertheless nothing but a succession of steep sidling pitches, creek fords, huge boulders, stumps, and almost impassable morasses, and taking it altogether, we are of the opinion that the Pueblo contributors to this road were badly

swindled; yet we believe that $1,000 more, judiciously expended upon it would make this a very fair road. . . .

Just before commencing the descent of the mountains the traveler suddenly comes in view of Wet Mountain Valley, spread out like a panorama. Just beyond and forming the west boundary of the valley are the lofty, rugged Wet Mountains [Sangre de Cristo Mountains], white with snow, which, with old Humboldt towering in their midst at least 12,000 feet above the level of the sea, give a grandeur to the landscape that must be seen to be appreciated.

This valley lies at an altitude of about 8,000 feet. It is forty miles long, and from four to six in width; this includes the valleys of Grape and Texas Creeks and their tributaries. It is better adapted to grazing and the raising of hay, barley, and potatoes, than anything else, although some wheat, oats, and garden stuff is raised in the most favored localities. So far as regards hay, this valley may be truthfully called the meadow of Colorado, and thousands of tons are cut annually. It contains a population of about six hundred, (they claim) among whom are a good many families of more than ordinary culture and refinement, and all seem well pleased with their location.

A lot changed after 1869, when settlers started pouring into the West Mountain Valley. When Edwin and George arrived in the valley in the late fall of 1869, the Ute Indians were still hunting atop the Wet Mountains, and the Beckwiths might have encountered their camps. The Ute had hunted in the Wet Mountains for thousands of years and had lived semi-peacefully with the frontiersmen who had come recently to hunt alongside them. Early White men who visited the valley included Spanish, French, and American fur trappers in the early to mid-nineteenth century and other Europeans who explored, hunted, and trapped in the area throughout the nineteenth century, including Kit Carson and John C. Fremont.

Around the time Edwin and George arrived, relations between the Ute and Whites were still peaceful. Interactions between the Ute and Arapahoe were not peaceful then, and settlers learned to avoid interference in skirmishes between the two tribes.

White intruders brought a new concept to the Native Americans—the curious notion that land could be owned and possessed by people. The Ute and Indigenous people in general believed that no one could own the land. It was provided to all by the Creator. This foreign concept would soon lead to misunderstandings, and mining in Colorado would ultimately lead to conflict.

In 1869, George and Edwin Beckwith most likely encountered Frank and George Kennicott. Originally from Illinois, the Kennicotts came to Colorado because they were suffering from tuberculosis. Like many tuberculosis sufferers, the Kennicotts found that the dry mountain climate helped improve their health. The Kennicotts had staked out 160-acre homesteads in the valley and were in the process of building a two-story log cabin, a homestead that still stands today. After its completion, they planned to return to Illinois to find wives and then come back to the valley to establish a cattle ranch and a freight business.

From the Kennicott place, George and Edwin might have seen construction to the south, where they would find the Davis family homesteading near the confluence of Taylor and Grape Creeks. Joseph Davis and his wife had originally built a log cabin, which they soon replaced with a larger, more

Figure 12: The Kennicott homestead, May 1910
Courtesy of the Old Westcliffe Schoolhouse Collection

comfortable home. Eventually they founded the first hotel
and general store in the valley.

A November 13, 1872, *Chieftain* article reported on Joseph
Davis's brother:

> Among the late arrivals is Mr. Chas. F. Davis, from
> Chicago, who we are glad to know has brought his wife
> [Elsie Chapin Davis, who would later marry Elton
> Beckwith] with him and proposes to stay. He is to form a
> business connection with the firm of [Joseph] Davis &
> Weston, merchants in this place.
>
> This firm commenced business at Ula about a year ago,
> and by their business-like dealings have established a
> good trade, and won the confidence of all the people of the
> valley. They have made quite a reduction from credit
> prices, and will sell all kinds of goods usually kept in a
> country store for cash or its equivalent only.

Edwin and George may have met or learned about some of the other pioneer settlers who had come to the valley with grit and dreams of building a life in this untamed wilderness. Elijah Horn was homesteading property at the base of the Sangre de Cristo range below what would come to be known as Horn Peak. He was a likeable character with a knack for tall tales. In the book *Custer County: Rosita, Silver Cliff, and Westcliffe*, Horn, in his later years, told of "how the antelope chased him into his cabin in the early days, and how the trout in Grape Creek collect along the bank by the hundreds as he approached the stream and would snatch the bait before it touches the water and try to pull him in!"

William Vorhis was homesteading land to the east and would establish a little town named Dora. In 1902, Dall DeWeese and C. R. C. Dye built a dam across Grape Creek so they could channel water to the property near Cañon City,

Figure 13: Homestead of John Hunter with beaver pelts on the wall. The Beckwiths probably encountered other Mountain Valley homesteads that looked like this.

Courtesy of the Westcliffe Old Schoolhouse Collection

named Fruitland. The reservoir formed by the dam became known as Lake DeWeese and covered the town of Dora.

George and Edwin must have noticed that the one thing all settlers seemed to share was the notion that the valley was perfect for cattle ranching. Edwin was eager to start his own business, so he and his father found good pastureland north of the Kennicotts' place and staked out 160 acre homesteads of their own.

Eager to get started and recognizing an opportunity, George and Edwin probably returned to Pueblo to record

Figure 14: Post card of Lake DeWeese with water flowing over the spillway, circa 1900
Courtesy of the Old Westcliffe Schoolhouse Collection

their homesteads.

It may seem like an impulsive decision, or perhaps it was an insightful vision, but George and Edwin purchased about four hundred head of cattle, starting a cattle speculation business that would eventually be named Beckwith & Sons. George and Edwin, probably with Goodnight's help, drove the cattle back to the Wet Mountain Valley. Then George headed back to the States, leaving Edwin in the valley, departing to Denver on December 10, 1869, per the Abraham Jacobs stagecoach line.

Could it be they were already planning to sell beef to miners, even though the boom was two years in the future? Since they had visited mining operations earlier in their journey in Central City and Georgetown, it is a possibility they speculated on a mining boom in the Wet Mountain Valley. Whatever their plan was at that point, it was the beginning of an incredibly successful cattle operation.

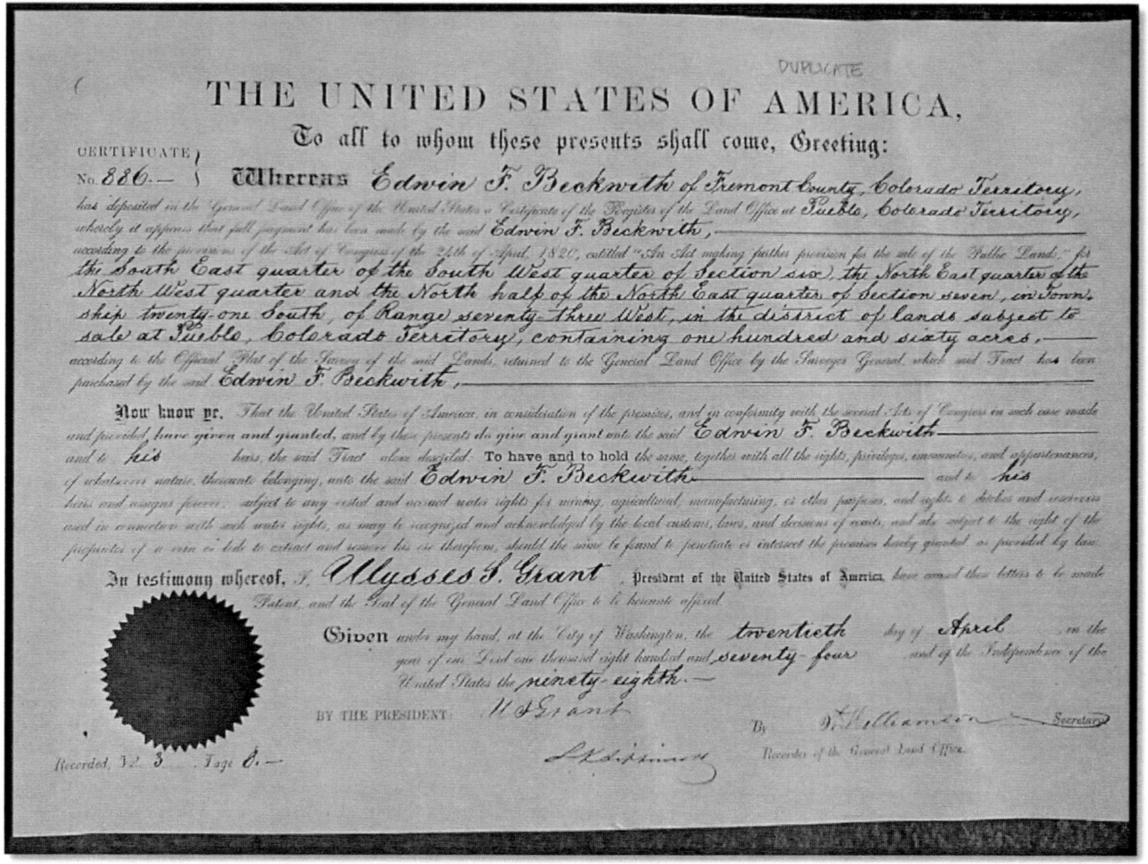

Figure 15: Edwin's homestead claim in the Wet Mountain Valley, signed by Ulysses S. Grant on April 20, 1874, approximately five years after Edwin homesteaded the land.

CHAPTER 5

Turning Point

The year 1870 was a turning point for the Beckwith family. Word of Edwin and George's trip to the Wet Mountain Valley circulated among members of the family. They apparently predicted that gold and silver would be discovered in the valley or there would be an opportunity to sell beef to miners and settlers throughout Colorado. It must have looked like a good business opportunity.

Edwin Beckwith stayed in the Wet Mountain Valley in Colorado, homesteading land and looking after the four hundred head of Texas longhorns he and his father had purchased.

George returned to his family and sold his home and businesses. He then moved with his wife and two younger daughters to Denver, Colorado, arriving on April 26, 1870, according to the *Rocky Mountain News*. In Denver he purchased a large mansion on Champa Street and began investing in local mines. Denver was a bustling, growing frontier town, and George began to establish a reputation as a successful capitalist. Unfortunately, Tamesin's health continued to fail, unaided by Colorado's healthy climate.

Elton was up against stiff competition with his flour and grain business in Philadelphia. Other such businesses flooded the market, so it was a tough business to make a profit. Elton sold the business and joined his brother in the Wet Mountain Valley. A September 2, 1872 affidavit signed by Edwin and William H. Phelps states that Elton settled on his own homestead on October 15, 1870 and made the Wet Mountain Valley his exclusive home from November 1, 1870, onward.

After his graduation from Harvard College in 1866, the oldest Beckwith brother, Loring, enrolled in Harvard Divinity School, graduating in 1870. On April 28, 1871, he married Alice Campbell Houghton. He was not interested in the cattle business, but the couple traveled to Denver, where in mid-May the *Rocky Mountain News* reported him giving sermons at the Unitarian church. On June 4, 1871, the *Rocky Mountain News* cited a letter in which Loring said he accepted "the invitation you extend to me, to unite with you in the establishment of a church of the Liberal Christian faith in Denver."

With both sons now in the cattle business, George established the Beckwith & Sons Cattle Investment Company, which financed and purchased more longhorn cattle, most likely from Charles Goodnight at his Rock Canyon Ranch. According to a report by a ranch hand, Willie Hendrickson, "Old man Beckwith and his two sons, Elton and Ed, brought several hundred head of Texas cattle, and turned them loose on the range." It was a bold move in anticipation of a market that had not yet developed in the valley by three men with no cattle ranching experience.

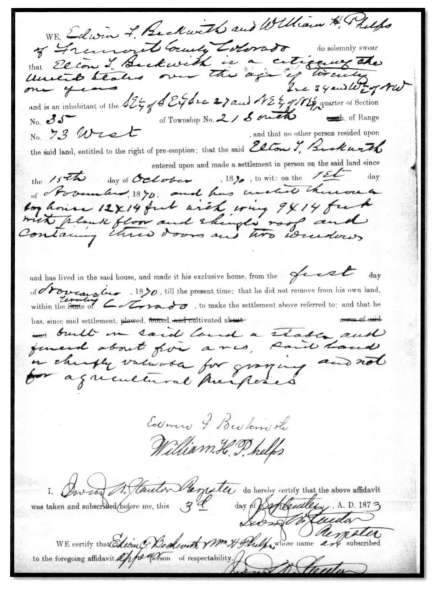

Figure 16: Affidavit signed on September 3, 1873, by
Edwin Beckwith and William H. Phelps verifying that
Elton Beckwith had arrived and settled in the Wet
Mountain Valley on October 15, 1870, building a twelve-
by fourteen-foot log house on his land.

Elton homesteaded 160 acres near Edwin and George's homesteads. Both sons and father executed land grants, signed by Ulysses S. Grant, awarded to them for their Civil War service, each for an additional 160 acres in the Wet Mountain Valley. These 960 acres (George, Edwin, and Elton each claimed two 160 acre land plots, one as a homestead and one for their Civil War service) were the start of the Beckwith

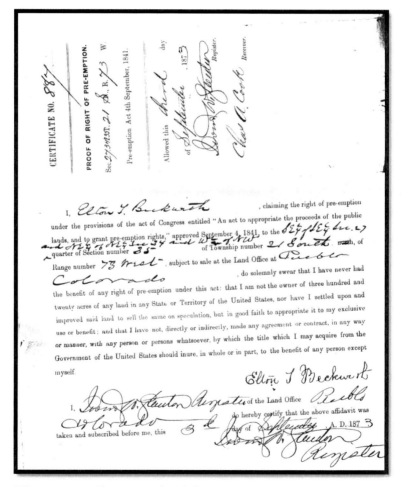

Figure 17: Elton Beckwith's September 3, 1873, proof of right of pre-emption document for land settled

Brother's Cattle Ranch that would eventually expand to become eighty-eight hundred acres. By the end of the century, it would be one of the largest and most successful ranches in Colorado.

Edwin's prediction was correct; their timing was perfect. Nine miles south of the Beckwiths' homesteads, in the foothills of the Wet Mountains, gold and silver were discovered near Rosita Hills in 1871. Miners began pouring into the Wet Mountain Valley, and the Beckwiths began selling beef as fast as they could acquire them.

Figure 18: Town of Rosita, circa 1875
Courtesy of the Old Westcliffe Schoolhouse Collection
Photographed by Chas. E. Emery

CHAPTER 6

The Valley Attracts Other Settlers

I n 1870, people began to arrive in the Wet Mountain Valley in significant numbers. A committee appointed by a group of German factory workers living in the Chicago area and organized by Carl Wulsten selected the Wet Mountain Valley as a site for colonization. Membership required good moral character, an age between twenty-one and forty-five, sound physical and mental health, and an investment of $250. *Harper's Weekly* reported on March 26, 1870, that the group was "accompanied by a clergyman, a doctor, and a schoolmaster, but as they intend to dwell in peace and unity, not by a lawyer."

They arrived in the Wet Mountain Valley in March 1870. The caravan of more than 250 people riding on and walking beside oxen-driven wagons with a full military escort would have been quite a spectacle for the lonesome valley. They entered the valley from the north and traveled up Copper Gulch, crossing the eastern edge of the Beckwiths' property.

Figure 19: Members of the German Colony head to Colorado as depicted in the March 26, 1870, *Harper's Weekly Journal of Civilization*

They continued on across the valley to the south and immediately established the town of Colfax, named after the US vice president, whom they had petitioned to issue a special group homestead land grant. Colfax and the German Colony were located in the south end of the valley, at the opposite end from the Beckwith properties.

The first thing the colony built was a dance floor. Then they laid out a town in square lots, which were issued to members by lottery. They set up a blacksmith shop, a townhouse, a little store, the doctor's tent, and a post office, which opened in May 1870. They planted a communal ten-acre garden and a wheat field. They had around a hundred head of cattle, a dozen milk cows, and a hundred goats. They established a brickyard and had brought machinery for a brewery.

According to the July 1870 US Census, there were 230 people living in the colony, including 171 foreign born individuals and 59 (mostly children) who were native born. Nearly one-third of the members were young men in their twenties who lived together three to a cabin.

Each family began building log cabins. In the book, *Custer County: Rosita, Silver Cliff, and Westcliffe*, author Joanne West Dodds details the experiences of one German settler:

> Colonist Barbara Falkenburg recalled her first home was an 8 by 10 foot structure with a slide board for a window. A packing box served as a cupboard. She and her husband had two blankets. She recalled, "we had very little meat and I never saw a pound of butter during the nine months time."

Soon the colony's troubles began. Constant disputes with the leader, Wulsten, led to the membership electing new officers in his absence in June. He would later say, according to Joanne West Dodds, "Whenever two Germans argue, there are three opinions."

Tragically, they got their crops in late, and then an early frost in August and a grasshopper swarm destroyed them. Very soon, money and supplies ran low. In December 1870, an explosion of a powder keg, probably caused by a defective fireplace, destroyed the store. The group's provisions, records, thirty-five Spencer rifles, and ammunition were lost. By April 1871, newspapers reported the venture a failure due to poor leadership and financial mismanagement. Many of the settlers eventually joined miners in Rosita or drifted away to Cañon City, Pueblo, or Denver. Some remained in the valley, with their descendants eventually settling in other areas of the Wet Mountain Valley.

In 1871, a number of Mormon families settled on land adjacent to that settled by the Germans near Taylor Creek. As reported in the *Rocky Mountain News* in February 1871, they were "not connected in any manner with the Utah outfit; being what are termed 'Josephites,' ignoring polygamy and the tithing system."

Dr. William A. Bell visited the valley with General William Jackson Palmer in 1870, searching for a southern railroad route. Bell was from England and came to the United States to study homeopathic medicine. He soon abandoned that to join Palmer's survey team to search for the best railroad route from Kansas to California. Bell and Palmer would form a lasting friendship while working on the survey and would one day have an immense impact on the Wet Mountain Valley.

Bell was so entranced by the beauty of the Wet Mountain Valley area that he bought a large tract of land. He partnered with Reginal Neave, a fellow Englishman, to purchase land for $40,000 in the center of the valley for the purpose of establishing a cheese factory. The cheese factory was initially successful. In an article in the *Colorado Daily Chieftain* on November 13, 1872, the authors reported visiting the cheese factory "and saw about 8,000 pounds of cheese which with a little more age will equal in quality, that of any other manufacture."

Tragically, Neave was murdered by Theodore D. T. Pryce, another Englishman and a prospective partner. Pryce, a noted knife thrower, threw a knife into Neave's forehead after a drinking binge that lasted three days.

Pryce came from wealthy English nobility. In spite of his impressive counsel and pressure on his behalf from the British government, he was sentenced to life imprisonment in the Cañon City territorial prison in 1874. After his appeals failed, he reportedly committed suicide by starving himself to death in 1882. Although his death was reported in the

Colorado Daily Chieftain on May 23, 1882, questions arose; some believed his death was staged. After his death, Englishmen living in the Wet Mountain Valley reported that Pryce had been sighted in England.

Pryce was one of many Englishmen who moved into the valley after 1871. Many Englishmen who came to the American West were "remittance men" or second sons. In England, the firstborn male inherited the family land, while sons further down the line might receive a remittance. Some of these English sons bought land in the Wet Mountain Valley as speculators and spent their time hunting and enjoying the beauty and the healthy climate. They invited friends from England to come to visit, hunt, and enjoy valley life with them. Many of these Englishmen settled around the Davis family homestead at the confluence of Grape and Taylor Creeks.

Joseph Davis and his wife were some of the earliest settlers in the valley. They had replaced their log cabin with a larger structure that served as their home, a mercantile, and a hotel for the newly founded town of Ula. When applying for a post office, Davis submitted the name Ure (pronounced "you-ray") in honor of the Ute chief Ouray, who with his people, had hunted in the Wet Mountain Valley long before any settlers, prospectors, or mountain men arrived.

Ouray and his wife, Chipeta, were highly respected in the valley because of their reputation as peace makers. In the 1870s, Utes were still hunting in the Wet Mountains despite the Ute Treaty of 1868 which made land west of the continental divide Ute territory. However, due to a clerical error, the postal administration misspelled the name on Davis's town submission's approval, recording it as Ula. The settlers stubbornly pronounced it *you-lay*. The Ula post office remained

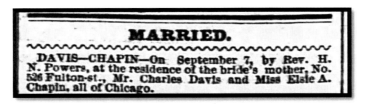

MARRIED.

DAVIS—CHAPIN—On September 7, by Rev. H.
N. Powers, at the residence of the bride's mother, No.
526 Fulton-st., Mr. Charles Davis and Miss Elsie A.
Chapin, all of Chicago.

**Figure 20: September 8, 1871, *Chicago Tribune*
announcement of the marriage of Charles Davis
and Elise A Chapin**

open for the following twenty years, but today only the Ula
Cemetery remains.

In 1871, Charles Davis married Elsie Chapin in Chicago
and the couple moved to the valley to join his family in Ula.
They established the Half Circle D Ranch near Ula, only a few
miles from the Beckwith Ranch.

In 1871, Frank and George Kennicott returned to Illinois,
where they both found wives. Frank married Mary Thorpe
and brought his new bride back to the ranch in the valley. In
August 1872, a daughter, Mary Louise Thorpe Kennicott, was
born in their two-story log cabin. Three days later, the mother
died of childbed fever and became the first person buried in
the Ula Cemetery. Today seven generations of the Kennicott
family are buried in the cemetery. Frank's mother-in-law took
the baby girl back to Canada.

Elton and Edwin Beckwith found an abandoned "one
room cabin, with a loft and high ceiling" the same year. The
cabin's original owners were named Horn and Taylor, two of
the valley's early settlers. The brothers took the cabin apart
and rebuilt it on property belonging to Elton, less than a mile
north of the Kennicotts' log cabin. According to Elton's
homestead proof, Elton also built stables near the cabin.

The Wet Mountain Valley was starting to bustle with
activity and the stage was set for vast changes.

CHAPTER 7

Gold and Silver Spark the Beckwith Fortune

Gold and silver were being discovered all around Colorado in the 1860s and 1870s. Ranchers in the Wet Mountain Valley, including the Beckwith brothers, believed it was only a matter of time before gold and precious metals would be discovered in their mountains.

Around 1860, George Skinner came to the Wet Mountain Valley from Illinois and was seen prospecting alone near what would later be named Horn Peak. He would occasionally turn up in Pueblo and Denver to buy supplies. Then, after 1863, he began appearing in Denver to not only buy supplies but also sell gold. Shortly afterward, his visits ceased. His letters to his brother also ceased. According to a November 25, 1938, article in the *Lake County Star*, his brother came to the valley to search for him and discovered an abandoned cabin below Horn Peak with "an old leather wallet, wound around with wire." Inside the wallet he found a letter written by George. The letter stated that George had found "a wonderfully rich mine." George's brother was unable to find George or the mine and eventually returned to Illinois.

In 1863, Joseph Doyle, who would go on to become a Colorado Territorial Council representative, proclaimed that he had discovered rich silver in the Wet Mountains a few days' ride from his Casa Blanca Ranch in Huerfano County, Colorado. Assay results on ore samples he produced showed that the ore was half silver. Before he staked a claim or reported the location of the find, he died of a heart attack in Denver.

Doyle's death started a search for his lost mine. Pueblo sheriff Si Smith, his brother Stephen, and two other friends found low-grade ore containing both gold and silver near the head of Grape Creek Canyon and Hardscrabble Creek. They established Smith's Mining District, ten miles square, in the Wet Mountains roughly ten miles east of Rosita Hills.

After Elijah Horn laid claim to land at the base of Horn Peak in 1869, George Skinner's brother returned to search again for George and the lost Skinner mine. This time he found the skeletal remains of his brother at the foot of a cliff in the Horn Peak area. Scattered around the skeleton were pieces of gold ore and George's diary, but although his brother returned to the area several times, he never found the Skinner mine. It remains lost today.

Possibly inspired by the lost Skinner mine, Elijah Horn started exploring in the Sangre de Cristos. While prospecting in the Crestone range, south of his homestead, he discovered a series of caves and caverns in Marble Mountain and Music Mountain, and below Milwaukee Peak. He probably believed he had found the site of the legendary La Caverna del Oro, the Cave of Gold.

Near the entrance to one of the caves, he found a large red Maltese cross painted on a rock wall. Legend has it that below the cave entrance were the crumbling remains of an old fort and, nearby, a decomposed skeleton in rusted conquistador armor. It is also said that a few miles south he found more Spanish implements. He never found signs of mining in the caverns, but he suspected the Spanish had explored there.

In June 1870, Richard Irwin, while passing through the valley on his way to New Mexico, was panning for gold and found some pieces of "good looking float." Irwin had his pieces assayed and decided to return to search for more. That same year, rancher Daniel Baker found minerals while searching for his cattle, but he just thought they were pretty and put them on the sill of his cabin window.

Irwin returned with Jasper Brown of Georgetown and convinced Baker to reveal where he had discovered his ore. He took them to Rosita Springs. Specimens found there produced some silver and gold but in insufficient quantities. In 1871, Louis Wilmer, formerly a member of the German Colony, found a few specimens on his ranch in Rosita Hills, but they assayed as being "not rich."

Irwin and W. J. Robinson founded the Hardscrabble Mining District on November 15, 1872. Their first claim was filed by Irwin in December 1872. The second claim, named the Senator, was filed with Irwin, Robinson, James Pringle, and V. B. Hoyt as claimants.

Irwin would later describe their first winter:

We would all go out and shoot at a mark for fun, and then have a dance on the cabin door, turned down on the floor for the occasion; James Pringle, Master of Ceremonies, who gave lessons in highland flings, Scotch reels and jig steps, on conditions that the rest of us would do the cooking, wash the dishes and chop the wood, which was cheerfully done, and thus rapidly and pleasantly passed the festive days away until winter was over, and Mr. Hoyt arrived with a disposition to rush things and now business meant work.

Word quickly spread, and soon mines started showing up and miners created a demand for beef. Miners, and all the society that came with them, flowed into the valley by the thousands. The town of Rosita was established. Today Rosita is a residential town roughly ten miles south of Westcliffe.

The Beckwith brothers were ready to capitalize on the opportunity and started selling beef as fast as they could acquire it. By 1886 Elton Beckwith was valued at 5 million (around $150 million in today's dollars).

After Rosita was founded, mining spread. In 1880, E. C.

Figure 21: The town of Rosita, 1879. On March 10, 1881, a fire destroyed much of Rosita.

Courtesy of the Old Westcliffe Schoolhouse Collection

Figure 22: Querida and the Bassick Mine
Courtesy of the Beckwith Ranch Collection
Photographed by Chas. E. Emery

Bassick established the little town of Querida, meaning "beloved" or "my dear," to service his massive Bassick Mine. It was one of Colorado's richest, deepest, and most advanced gold mines for its time (1877-1885). Today only foundations remain in the ghost town of Querida, ten miles northeast of Rosita and twelve miles east of Westcliffe.

On January 27, 1878, after the discovery of silver ores ten miles northwest of the Bassick gold mine, the town of Silver Cliff was established. Silver mining in the vicinity of Rosita, Querida and Silver Cliff brought several thousand prospectors into the region. By the end of the decade, Silver Cliff boasted a population of more than five thousand, becoming the third largest town in Colorado.

During this time, William Bell and William Jackson Palmer formed the Denver & Rio Grande Railway. By late October 1871, the railway was completed from Denver to Colorado Springs, a town founded by Palmer in 1871.

Bell and Palmer also founded the town of Manitou Springs just west of Colorado Springs in 1872, intending the town to be a scenic health resort. Bell conducted a campaign to promote the health benefits of the resort's water, earning it the nickname "Saratoga of the West," after Saratoga Springs in New York.

That year, Bell married Cara Scovell in England and came back to build their Victorian home, Briarhurst Manor, on the banks of Fountain Creek in Manitou Springs. Wealthy easterners and English investors poured into Manitou Springs and Colorado Springs, building luxury hotels, parks, and shops. They brought with them their penchant for afternoon tea and English sports. Colorado Springs would come to be known as Little London.

In 1872, Palmer and Bell completed railroad tracks to Pueblo and to the Florence coal fields. Then they added a spur from Colorado Springs to Manitou Springs. It was said of the rapid expansion of the D&RG that "the Rio Grande would cheerfully build a branch line to Hades if brimstone traffic looked promising." Therefore, it was no surprise that the D&RG soon turned its attention to the mining and ranching activity in the Wet Mountain Valley.

CHAPTER 8

The Waverly Ranch

In 1873, Elton and Edwin Beckwith were mourning the loss of their mother, Tamesin, in Denver. It was a difficult time, but Elton was about to meet the woman who would change his life.

Also in 1873, only two years after Charles Davis established the Half Circle D Ranch near Ula, he died. His widow, Elsie Chapin Davis, had grown up accustomed to the finer things and was college educated. It is clear that the Wet Mountain Valley, although beautiful, did not meet her expectations.

The year after Charles' death, Elton Beckwith began courting Elsie. He might have been proud of the log cabin he and Edwin had rebuilt on the Beckwith property, but Elsie must not have been impressed because Elton began several improvements. Probably with Edwin's help, Elton raised the roof and built a huge bedroom and a small nursery, replacing the loft of the cabin. Downstairs, he split the large room into

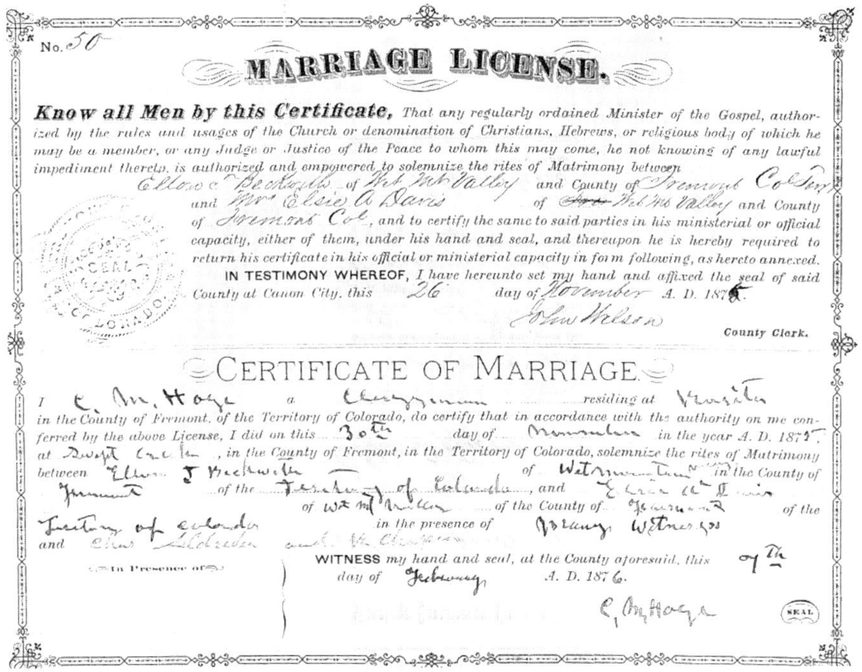

No. 50

MARRIAGE LICENSE.

Know all Men by this Certificate, That any regularly ordained Minister of the Gospel, authorized by the rules and usages of the Church or denomination of Christians, Hebrews, or religious body of which he may be a member, or any Judge or Justice of the Peace to whom this may come, he not knowing of any lawful impediment thereto, is authorized and empowered to solemnize the rites of Matrimony between Elton C Beckwith of Wet Mt Valley and County of Fremont Col Ter and Mrs Elsie A Davis of Wet Mt Valley and County of Fremont Col, and to certify the same to said parties in his ministerial or official capacity, either of them, under his hand and seal, and thereupon he is hereby required to return his certificate in his official or ministerial capacity in form following, as hereto annexed.

IN TESTIMONY WHEREOF, I have hereunto set my hand and affixed the seal of said County at Canon City, this 26 day of November A. D. 1875.

John Wilson
County Clerk.

CERTIFICATE OF MARRIAGE.

I C. M. Hoge a Clergyman residing at Rosita in the County of Fremont, of the Territory of Colorado, do certify that in accordance with the authority on me conferred by the above License, I did on this 30th day of November in the year A. D. 1875, at Dwight Creek, in the County of Fremont, in the Territory of Colorado, solemnize the rites of Matrimony between Elton J Beckwith of Wet Mountain Valley in the County of Fremont of the Territory of Colorado, and Elsie A Davis of Wet Mt Valley of the County of Fremont of the Territory of Colorado in the presence of Henry Wetmore and Chas Schroeder

In Presence of

WITNESS my hand and seal, at the County aforesaid, this 7th day of February A. D. 1876.

C. M. Hoge

SEAL

Figure 23: Marriage license of Elton and Elsie Beckwith

a parlor and a study. Evidently, Elsie was satisfied, and she married Elton on November 30, 1875.

After his brother's marriage, Edwin Beckwith built his own small cabin on his homestead. His 1881 homestead proof stated, "My first house was built in 1875. I built another in 1876, it is one story. The main building is 24' x 22'. Also have outbuildings and corrals."

Elsie loved to entertain and have parties, so she encouraged Elton to expand the log cabin by adding a large dining room and kitchen. Legend has it that the kitchen was large and included a dining table because Elsie would not allow cowboys working on the Beckwith Ranch to eat in her fine dining room.

In keeping with the styles Elton had been accustomed to in Maine, and after having learned of Elsie's penchant for

Victorian architecture and style, he covered the log cabin and new rooms with white clapboard siding and painted the roof bright red. The new additions enabled Elsie to invite the wives of the English remittance men over for high tea at precisely 4 p.m. every day. She also invited some of the other ladies in the valley, but if they did not meet her standards, they might not get invited back.

The Beckwiths hired staff to cook and handle the domestic chores. They built a large scullery where staff could clean clothes, wash dishes, sew, and perform other mundane chores. The outside walls of the additions were also covered with white clapboard siding to continue the Victorian look.

Figure 24: Elsie Beckwith with Herbie. They are sitting in the Beckwith front parlor, undated photo
Courtesy of the Beckwith Ranch Collection

**Figure 25: One of the earliest known pictures of the
Beckwith Ranch, circa 1890. It was taken before the *porte
cochère* (carriage porch) was added.**
Courtesy of the Beckwith Ranch Collection

The Beckwiths also had aspen and cottonwood trees planted
behind the house. Elsie named their home the Waverly Ranch.
It is unknown why she chose the name, but for many years,
the current Beckwith Ranch was known as the Waverly
Ranch.

It is clear that Elsie Beckwith yearned to make Waverly
Ranch the center of the English lifestyle that was flourishing
in Manitou Springs, Colorado Springs, and the English homesteads of the Wet Mountain Valley.

Elsie's high standards made her appear to be a snob to
most of the ranching families in the valley, but she kept up a

good relationship with her neighbors the Kennicotts. Anna Kennicott and her daughter Eugenia visited Elsie at Waverly Ranch often, and Elsie visited the Kennicott house as well.

Anna was a graduate of Stanford University where she majored in classic languages and chemistry, so she had good credentials. Eugenia was an invalid all her life, having contracted spinal tuberculosis at age two. She triumphed over her disability with a strong will, and when she was sixteen, in 1899, her father gave her a camera. She took many photographs of her family, the Wet Mountain Valley, and some of the Beckwiths and their ranch. She had a keen eye for composition.

Evidence of Anna and Elsie's close friendship is noted by Marcia Drager, one of the granddaughters of the Kennicotts, who continues to live on the Kennicott homestead. When Elsie replaced her dining table, she gave the old one to the Kennicotts, and it remains there today. Marcia donated a baby dress that Elsie gave to one of the Kennicotts as a wedding or baby gift. The Friends of Beckwith Ranch have put the dress on display inside the ranch.

A diary kept by Eugenia Kennicott's sister Anna in 1899 gives a snapshot of life in the valley as seen by an eleven-year-old young girl. It makes it clear that the Beckwiths, Kennicotts, and Davises (Elsie's in-laws) were good friends and enjoyed each other's company. When Elton Beckwith died, Mr. F. L. Kennicott was one of his pallbearers. When Elsie died, Eugenia Kennicott was a beneficiary in her will.

While Elsie created society in the valley, Elton and Edwin were embracing the ranching and cowboy lifestyle.

CHAPTER 9

Cowboy Life—The Roundup

In 1876, the one-hundred-year anniversary of the signing of the Declaration of Independence, the United States was still divided into the settled East and the frontier West, separated by the ninety-eighth meridian. Colorado was well west of the meridian.

The American frontier, also called the Old West, or Wild West, could be said to have begun with the Louisiana Purchase in 1803 or perhaps around 1862 with the Homestead Act. It ended with the admission of the last western territories as states in 1912. During this era of massive migration and settlement, the cowboy became a symbol of the American West.

The cowboy life required completely different skills from working in shipbuilding or the merchant marines, but it is clear that George Beckwith and his sons Elton and Edwin were irresistibly attracted to and embraced it. George Beckwith invested heavily in cattle speculation with his sons and built his own two-thousand-acre ranch near the town of Longmont (northwest of Denver), and at the same time, Elton and Edwin built a ranching dynasty in the Wet Mountain Valley.

Ranch owners typically hired an experienced ranch foreman to manage their cattle herds, but Elton and Edwin initially chose to manage their ranch and cattle themselves. In addition to a ranch foreman, the large cattle operation needed a cook, cowboys, broncobusters, and wranglers.

Elton Beckwith hired only the best for the Waverly Ranch. In the late 1880s and through the 1890s, Milt Raper was the cook at the ranch and kept the cowboys and ranch hands well fed. For a typical meal, Milt spread out a large rubber mat on the grass and covered it with tin dishes for the ranch hands. He then served a big plate of steaks, plenty of butter, and hot rolls called Sour Dough Punk, said to be "as fine as any you can get in a first class bakery." There were also beans, corn, tomatoes, and dried fruit served with hot coffee.

It is likely that the coffee served on the Beckwith Ranch was Arbuckles' Ariosa. In 1871, John Arbuckle invented a machine that filled paper bags with coffee and then weighed, sealed, and labeled them. Packaged in his factory in New York, Arbuckles' Ariosa was the first mass-produced coffee sold nationwide. Arbuckles' coffee became a staple for pioneers across the frontier.

During the 1870s and 1880s, there were few fences in the valley, so Beckwith cattle ranged free, mixing with cattle owned by other ranchers. Ranchers distinguished their cattle by branding them. The Beckwith brand looked like a slanted T and was often referred to as the Lazy T.

Ranch cowboys followed the herd, so that its whereabouts were known when it was time for the roundup. They also discouraged cattle thieves. Sometimes, they were accompanied by a cook with a chuck wagon, a western mobile kitchen.

Mobile kitchens had been around for many years, but Charles "Chuck" Goodnight invented the chuck wagon in 1866. He modified a Studebaker-manufactured covered wagon, a durable Civil War army surplus wagon, to better suit long cattle drives. He added a "chuck box" to the back of the wagon, with drawers, shelves, and a hinged lid serving as a table or work surface. The chuck wagon carried a water barrel, firewood, cooking utensils, supplies, and cowboys' personal items.

In early spring, cows gave birth to their calves. The Beckwith brothers brought in a crew of cowboys to prepare for the spring roundup. Each cowboy required a string of horses, so in May an experienced broncobuster was hired to break and train fresh horses. The Beckwith brothers made sure only the best cowboys came to Waverly Ranch. They brought in these tough and hardy cowboys after they had made a name for themselves elsewhere in the West.

Famous cowboys who broke horses at the Waverly Ranch include Scot McComb, from Bear River, Colorado; Charlie Right, from Wyoming; and Willie Hendrickson, whose grandfather George W. Vorhis was one of the first settlers in the Wet Mountain Valley. Vorhis arrived around 1869, the same year Edwin Beckwith homesteaded in the valley.

In 1941, Willie Hendrickson was persuaded by his ninety-five-year-old mother to write about his experiences as a broncobuster. The following excerpt from his unpublished manuscript describes his work at the Beckwith Ranch in 1890:

Well the next morning [after arriving at Waverly Ranch], the boss [Elton Beckwith] and I saddled up two old saddle horses and went over in the pasture and got about one hundred head of horses, mares and colts. He picked out six big fat six-year old horses for me to break. Those six-year old horses look pretty tough to me. He had not had any broke for two years, so you see it left me a pretty shaky bunch to break. They sure looked pretty wild and as wild as a deer. Well we ran one in the circle corral, caught him by the front feet first—troughed him on his side, put on a scotch hobble and then let him up. I put on my saddle, and then got up on his back. He sure done a good job of it [bucking]. All the cowboys sat on the fence to see the fun. Well I rode him easy. I had rode lots of bad horses, but never as a business before. Of course, I naturally would feel sorter shaky, but that soon wore off.

I guess I will tell you how we do the job. We run a wild bronco in the circle corral, and as he runs around the corral, we catch him by the front feet, rare back on the rope and he goes spinning through the air, and lights on his side. A cowboy falls on him, puts his knees on his neck, then takes him by the nose and turns him nose up. (Holding to it.)

You then take your rope and put it around his neck. Making a collar. Then take the rope and put it around his hind foot making it short enough so he cannot get his hind foot to the ground. Then let him up. He can't do a thing. Can't kick you or hardly move. He is under your control. Then put on your saddle. Take the scotch hobble off, and turn him loose in the corral. He will do his best bucking with the saddle. Then catch him and he is ready to ride.

Typically each cowboy had six to eight horses to use in the spring roundup and later in the fall for the cattle drive to market.

Despite its name, spring roundup typically occurred around June 15. Each ranching outfit set up camp at a designated location in the valley. Each cowboy brought their string of well-trained cow horses. The cowboys had an evening feast, and since each outfit had a cook, there were many tents set up. That night the cowboys bedded down early to get plenty of sleep and rose before sunup the next day.

The cowboys scattered out to comb the valley for cows and their new calves and then drove them back to the appointed location. There could be two or three thousand head bunched together there.

Each outfit then cut out its cattle by brand and bunched them together to brand the new calves. The Beckwith brand was the Lazy T, although the 1899 *Custer County Cattle Growers' Association Brand Book* also lists the Half Circle D brand, indicating that Elton continued to run his wife's former ranch and use her brand long after their marriage.

Figure 26: The 1899 *Custer County Cattle Growers' Association Brand Book* **showing the Beckwith brand, the lazy T, on the cow's backside and Elsie's first husband's brand, the Half Circle D**

Figure 27: Roundup near the Beckwith Ranch, circa 1880
Courtesy of the Beckwith Ranch Collection
Photographed by Chas. E. Emery

One year the Beckwiths were accused of branding other ranchers' calves. When questioned, one rancher quipped to the *Wet Mountain Tribune*, "It seems strange that the Beckwiths always have a 110% calving rate when the rest of us only get about 80%." Because of this, some ranchers started their roundups earlier so that the Beckwiths would not have a chance to brand their calves.

After branding, each outfit drove its cattle back to its ranch for summer feeding. In the fall, the cattle were driven to market. Throughout the summer, cowboys continued rounding up cattle that were missed in the first roundup. These late finds were taken back to the ranch to be branded and included with the herd.

It was hoped that the new calves would get fat and healthy grazing on the fertile grasses of the sub-irrigated valley floor in time to be shipped to market in the fall.

CHAPTER 10

Rustling—The Beckwiths and McCoys

L iving next to Wild West mining towns filled with hungry and rugged miners had its advantages and disadvantages. It provided a ready market for beef but also brought in rowdy, desperate men searching for an easy buck. The local sheriffs were kept busy dealing with claim jumpers, gunfights, bar room brawls, and endless disputes. They had little time for tracking down cattle thieves. That job often fell upon the ranchers themselves, as evidenced in the following article from the *Sierra Journal*, published in Rosita on November 22, 1883:

> Elton Beckwith, the chief of good fellows and cattle king of Custer County, was in town Monday. He had just returned from a trip through Park and Elpaso [El Paso] counties after fifteen head of horses that was stolen from him last winter and succeeded in recovering nine head of them and will probably get the other six after a while. He

is on the trail of both the horses and thief and will hunt
them down.

Another article, published in the *Herald Democrat* on
November 5, 1892, tells of Edwin's adventures with cattle
thieves:

> Several years ago [in the 1880s] there was a gang of rus-
> tlers known as the McCoy gang in central Colorado that
> robbed the cattlemen right and left. So bold did they be-
> come that tenderloin steaks were sold in Coropal [Coto-
> paxi?] for a cent a pound. It was through the efforts of
> [Edwin] Beckwith that the gang was practically annihi-
> lated, and that Dick McCoy, one of the worst desperadoes
> ever unhung, is now "doing life" at Canyon City.
>
> But for Beckwith's story. "It was in October of 1888,"
> began he, "that I found Fred Arnold dead on Texas Creek.
> Arnold was one of our riders, you know. There was a big
> hole in his breast, and his legs were riddled with Winches-
> ter bullets. Both of his guns were in his belt. I knew that
> Arnold was a quick man with a gun and that he must have
> been ambushed. As a matter of fact he rode the western
> range because we knew him to be a fighter and able to take
> care of himself in any trouble he might have with the
> McCoy gang.
>
> "A quick search showed tracks from a couple of men
> and horses behind the willows on the other side of the
> creek. The trail of one of the men revealed that he had
> dragged his left leg a trifle. That meant Dick McCoy sure.
> After following the trail of the horses for five miles, and
> seeing that it pointed to the McCoy ranch, I turned back
> and picked poor Arnold up and took him to the [Beck-

with] ranch. The verdict of the coroner's jury was 'Murdered by persons unknown.' It's the regulation form, but it didn't suit us. So we called a meeting of the cattlemen and talked it over. It didn't take long to come to the conclusion that if we wanted to protect our interests and save the lives of our riders and ourselves the McCoy gang had to be wiped out.

"In the early morning two days later sixteen men rode through the gulch that ended at McCoy's place. There wasn't any shelter, and we had to ride for it. In the corral were seven men killing rustled cattle. On the fence were half a dozen hides with the brands cut out. The sight made us crazy, and with a yell we dashed forward. The rustlers 'cut loose' first and two of our men dropped out of their saddles. One was killed, the other shot through the shoulder. We got six of the seven. The seventh was old Dick McCoy, whom I winged as he was trying to hide behind a cow. The rustlers in the ranch skipped out when they saw how it was going. Peg Leg Smith and a couple of others who got away are now doing time at Canon City for robbing a Denver and Rio Grande express train.

"We didn't kill McCoy and put him out of his misery, but thought he'd suffer more if he was patched up and sentenced for life for half a dozen murders. He's enjoying himself in a tennis suit in the 'pen' in Canon City now."

The Beckwith brothers were instrumental in forming the Wet Mountain Valley Cattlemen's Association, a group that often dealt with cattle rustlers. Typically, when a rustler was captured, he was taken before the local judge. For those found guilty, the punishment at the time was death by hanging. The cattlemen would take care of the execution themselves, often hanging the rustler from the horse barn at Elton Beckwith's ranch.

The execution would be advertised, with the community invited to attend. Elton and Elsie Beckwith would sponsor a grand party for the event, with bands playing atop the *porte cochère* and a feast with plenty of drinks. The "necktie party," was intended to discourage anyone thinking about rustling cattle.

The following is an account by Wet Mountain Valley resident Wildra Walker about just such an event. Walker wrote a series of articles published in the *Wet Mountain Tribune* titled "Tales from the Old Times." This is "Bridget's Story," published on July 30, 2009:

> Little Bridget Burns was only fourteen years old when, in the year 1878, she and her family, with several other families, optimistically arrived at the north end of the Wet Mountain Valley. It had been a long, hard, arduous journey from somewhere in Missouri. The little group of horse-drawn wagons was finally close to its destination where the men hoped to make their fortune in the silver

Figure 28: The Beckwith Ranch with the *porte cochère* where bands played on the rooftop
Courtesy of the Filter Press Collection

mining boom that had exploded in the hills around Silver Cliff. The road, hardly more than a trail wound up, through and around hills, valleys and cliffs which somewhat follows present day Highway 69 from Texas Creek, had taken a toll on both beasts and humans, so when the narrow, difficult trail widened out onto the broad, level expanse of the Valley, all were relieved. Spirits lifted, then soared to new heights when the party saw in the near distance (at the Beckwith Ranch location), a large gathering of some kind. Buggies, wagons, saddle horses were grouped together, and the crowd of people that was milling about seemed to be a part of some special occasion—a picnic, perhaps. And judging from the bonfires and savory odors of barbecuing meats it looked, to the weary travelers so near the end of a difficult journey like a joyous community-minded affair. . . .

Suddenly, the scene took a shocking and horrific turn. There, in the midst of the festivities, was a crudely constructed gallows, and from this a man was hanging. The picnic was incidental to the event which had drawn the crowd—a public lynching. Bridget, with the group of newly arrived pioneers, had unexpectedly come face to face with grim reality. The code of the West was harsh. Justice was swift and violent.

Bridget always lamented as she told this story that she could not understand how those ordinary people could callously find gratification in the death, at their own hands, of a fellow human being, even though by all standards, he was a rascal. One thing she did understand—it had been made perfectly clear—a crime that was not tolerated in this early ranching community was cattle rustling.

CHAPTER 11

The Cowboy Life — Cattle Drive and Harness Racing

Most of the Beckwiths' cattle supplied beef to the miners, but the surplus was sold at different city markets. Before the Denver & Rio Grande Western Railroad came to Westcliffe in 1881, the cattle had to be driven to Texas Creek to be sold to non-valley markets. Around the last of October, Beckwith cowboys prepared to drive cattle to the stockyards at Texas Creek on the Arkansas River. From there they were loaded on the train to Cañon City, where they were transferred to a train bound for Kansas City.

The big drive to Texas Creek started at sunrise, and it took most of the first day to reach Indian Springs Park, about fifteen miles north of Waverly Ranch. Typically they arrived a little after noon, and the steers were allowed to graze on Indian Spring Park pasture until sundown, when they were put in a large corral for the night.

The cook and chuck wagon were there with a big supper. The men built two big bonfires on opposite sides of the corral, and two cowboys at a time rode around the corral talking and singing to the cattle to keep them quiet and to keep coyotes and other predators away.

Daylight the next morning, the cattle were released from the corral. This was a dangerous event since Texas longhorn cattle were far from tame or docile and would charge out of the corral. If anyone got in their way, they might hook the cowboy's horse with their long horns.

The cowboys drove the cattle down the valley to the railroad stockyards on the Arkansas River, arriving late in the evening. They held the cattle there until the next morning, when they were loaded on cars and taken to Cañon City for shipment.

The following is a story about one of these cattle drives told by Willie Hendrickson:

> I will tell you about another time when we had about five hundred head of steers in this same corral [at Indian Spring Park]. The boss [Elton Beckwith] said that he believed that he would not have us stand guard that night. He said he didn't think they would get scared, and that he would take a chance.
>
> We all saddled a good horse and tied him to the wagon, which was about ten feet from our bed. We did this so we would be ready in case of a stampede. This happened on the night of November the second, 1892, at just ten minutes after two o'clock, according to the cook clock. While we were all snoring, and taking our ease, a sound like thunder awoke every man. The big stampede was on. Every man ran for his horse, every cowboy in his place.

Racing through the darkness, they sounded like thunder as they ran. On and on they ran, like demons in the night. Once in a while you could see a cowboy as he rode down through the darkness. On and on in the night. One hour passed and still they ran. Our horses were getting tired. Once in a while, we could see each other riding just in front of those wild monsters. Just twenty feet from terrible death should a horse fall while racing through the darkness.

Two hours passed, and still they ran. Suddenly, I heard a voice, it was Beckwith. Way off in the darkness he shouted in a very loud voice, "Swing them to the left, boys." Quicker than a flash of a pistol, we made a dash through the night and swung these leaders just far enough to keep them from plunging down a deep canyon. If we had not succeeded in turning them, they would have plunged over a steep precipice into a deep canyon and steers would have been piled up, probably two hundred feet deep. Beckwith might have lost the whole bunch.

By that time, we had them on the edge of Indian Spring park. They were still running and bawling as the sign of day light appeared in the east. We now could see more what we were doing and we began to circle them on this big park. This was done by all the cowboys got on one side of the herd and began to crowd the leaders. In a short time, we had them running in a circle and the more we crowded the leaders, the smaller the circle.

As it began to get lighter, I saw a cowboy and heard him moan. It was Scot McComb. He was nearly frozen to his saddle. You see, when the cattle broke some two and one half hours before, he jumped from his bed and grabbed his chaps. He did not take any time to put on any pants or any socks. Just his chaps and boots and hat and spurs. No coat. Well, we sent a cowboy to take him to camp and as quick as he had a couple of slices of bread and a cup of coffee and a hunk of meat, he was okay. Well, we finally got them to the railroad.

That night they broke the Denver & Rio Grande railroad stock yard down and they all got away. Beckwith's contract with the buyer was to deliver them in the stockyards. Beckwith got all of his money, but Mr. Wolf lost heavily, as he had to hire Cotlan's cowboys to round them up for him.

From the 1860s through the 1890s, cowboys were mostly just young men and boys needing cash. The average cowboy in the West during this time earned about $25 to $40 a month. No record has been found of the racial mix at Waverly Ranch, but typically forty-five percent of the cowboys of this era were black, Hispanic, mixed race, or Indian. Records and articles from the ranch contain details of two black brothers, Bill and Ben Boyer, who worked at the Beckwith Ranch from around 1890 to 1895. According to John Stokes Holley in his book, *The Invisible People of the Pikes Peak Region*, Bill was said to be "about the best rider on the job" and a noted quick draw. For a time, there was also a Ute cowboy who went by the name Terry. Although cowboys were primarily involved in herding and branding cattle, they also cared for horses and repaired fences, corrals, and the barns.

As the Waverly Ranch grew, Elton and Edwin added dairy cows and racehorses to their livestock. They also added a horse barn, dairy barn, blacksmith shed, calving barn, and bunkhouse.

Most ranchers produced an excess of milk, cream, and cheese to sell in the town for extra income. However, even

Figure 29: Undated historical photo of the Beckwith Ranch showing the numerous outbuildings

Courtesy of the Beckwith Ranch Collection

though the Beckwiths had a large dairy barn and plenty of milk cows, they produced only enough dairy products for use on the ranch.

Elton Beckwith also kept a small number of ranch hands and a blacksmith at the headquarters to tend to the dairy operation; maintain and repair tack, wagons, and buildings; and haul supplies from town in wagons. He also hired wranglers to care for the prize racehorses. The June 13, 1907, *Wet Mountain Tribune* wrote, "Both brothers leaned toward fine horses, and the Beckwith racing string acquired a national reputation."

Elton Beckwith loved harness racing and kept some of the finest trotters in Colorado. Two of his horses, Lady Belle and Kingston, won many races, but his favorite champion trotter was named Creedmore. Trotters were standardbred horses; their shorter legs made them good for trotting races.

Harness racing had been around since the 1820s in America. Ranchers and wealthy horsemen enjoyed earning bragging rights and competed against one another. Early races took place on homemade racetracks, country roads, and village streets. In the Wet Mountain Valley, harness racing was a major event at local community celebrations and fairs. The valley's original racetrack is still visible in a satellite image, showing it was east of today's Silver Cliff Park.

Racing trotters began with riders on saddles but evolved into pulling wagons and sulkies. The greater speed available from a sulky made it the most favored vehicle in harness racing. The high-wheeled sulky became popular in the mid-1800s. In 1878, the bent axle allowed the use of shorter shafts and made a more compact and stable vehicle. In 1892, wooden wheels were replaced by tires like those used on bicycles. The "bike-sulky" greatly increased the potential

Figure 30: Satellite image showing signs of the old racetrack near Silver Cliff Park

speed of the trotter.

During the 1890s the Beckwith mansion expanded with the addition of a downstairs entryway, a ballroom, and a rounded wraparound porch. Upstairs additions were a large bedroom for Velma, a large corridor, and a bathing room containing a claw-foot tub and toilet.

Elsie and Velma built quite a reputation for their refined taste, filling the mansion with fine furnishings and decor from their many trips around the world.

Figure 31: This is believed to be Creedmore, Elton
Beckwith's prize standardbred stallion. Creedmore
was described in a front-page article in the *Silver Cliff
Rustler* on September 28, 1904.
Courtesy of the Beckwith Ranch Collection

Nothwithstanding some of the best
horses in Colorado were on exhibition
at the Fremont county fair, Hon. Elton Beckwith's fine standard-bred
stallion, Creedmore, was awarded first
prize in two features, taking first in
the show of roadsters three years of
age and older and sweepstakes in the
exhibit of stallions any age or breed.
Mr. Beckwith is quite proud of having
carried off these honors at the fair,
and it will afford all our residents who
feel county pride, pleasure to learn of
his success.

CHAPTER 12

Custer County and the Wet Mountain Valley

According to Elton and Elsie Beckwith's marriage license, they were married in Fremont County at Swift Creek in 1875. Swift Creek originates above Lake of the Clouds in the Sangre de Cristo Mountains, between Spread Eagle and Mount Marcy Peaks. The stream flows through Lake of the Clouds into the valley and runs through the old Swift Ranch; hence its name. It originates as snowmelt but is fed by springs along its journey as it passes behind the Waverly Ranch to join Grape Creek before flowing into Lake DeWeese and eventually the Arkansas River.

Before 1877, the Wet Mountain Valley was part of Fremont County in the Colorado Territory. On March 3, 1875, the US Congress passed an act specifying the requirements for Colorado to become a state. On August 1, 1876, four weeks after the centennial of the United States, President Ulysses S.

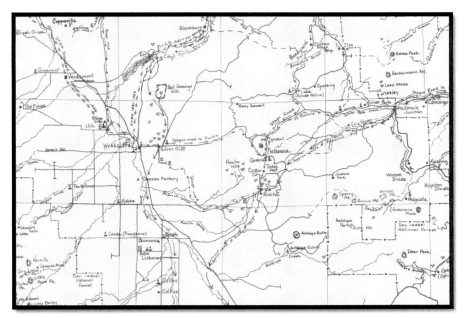

Figure 32: Historical map showing the Beckwith Ranch in relation to Westcliffe, Silver Cliff, and Rosita
Courtesy of History Colorado, Accession #G4313.C8S1.1800-1982.H5
Drawn by Nancy Colvin Hirleman

Grant signed a proclamation admitting Colorado to the Union as the thirty-eighth state, making it the "Centennial State."

Named in honor of General George Armstrong Custer, Custer County was created in 1877 from what had been the southern portion of Fremont County; the northern portion remained Fremont County.

The county seat was in Ula from 1872 through 1878, but as Rosita grew in size, the county seat moved there. In 1885, the county seat was moved to Silver Cliff and finally to Westcliffe in 1928.

The Beckwiths were doing quite well when Elsie gave birth to their daughter and only child, Elsie Velma, around 1878.

By 1876, Elsie's mother, Polly, and her three brothers, Oscar, Edmund (Ed), and Rufus, had moved to the Wet Mountain Valley. They all homesteaded land and eventually sold their homesteads to Elton and Edwin.

Elsie's brothers worked on the Beckwith Ranch, which may explain why they sold their homesteads to Elton for low prices. In 1876, Rufus sold his 160 acres to Elton for $1. In 1879, Elton paid Ed $200 for his 160-acre homestead. In 1881, Polly sold Elton 160 acres for $500. Ed sold another 160 acres to Elton for $550 in 1883.

Today Rosita and Querida are residential communities with little sign of the large mining towns they once were. Silver Cliff is still a small town sitting next to Westcliffe and has its own town government. However, Silver Cliff's population shrunk from 5,000 in 1880 to around 609 in 2020, according to the 2020 US Census. Westcliffe's population in the 2020 census was 435, while that same census reported the Custer County population at 4,704. Despite its low population, Westcliffe continues to be the county seat.

From 1887 through 1890, Theodore D. A. Cockerell, born in London, lived in the Wet Mountain Valley with the Cusack family, in the resort currently known as the Pines Ranch. He later became head of the Botany Department at the University of Colorado at Boulder. In one of his letters, he wrote his impressions of the Wet Mountain Valley of that time:

> Most of the people are employed in mining or ranching and are a very rough lot on the whole. Law, as understood in England, does not exist, and C. S. Cox says it is as easy to buy over a judge as to buy one's dinner. Lynching is not very rare, and if a man is killed usually nothing worse happens to his murderer than that he has to leave Colorado. Still, there is probably more fellow-feeling among

these people than in England and they will do much to help one another, though they will also swindle each other to any extent when they get the chance. Horses sometimes get stolen, but petty thieving is extremely rare, and we can leave our cabin with door open for days without much fear of anything being stolen.

In a later letter, he wrote:

There is no doubt that ranch life, if hard for the men, is doubly so for the women unless there are two or three in the house. All the small farmsteads are called ranches. The word "farm" is hardly ever used. Settlers nearly always take a plot (about 200 acres) allowed them by the government. They build a small log hut, often with only one apartment, and spend their capital in the purchase of cattle, pigs, potatoes and seed, and generally get also a horse and a gun. Others, like Cox, having a little more money, buy a ranch with a house, barn already built. The owner nearly always works on his ranch and generally only hires his labor when harvesting, which needs extra hands. . . . Wages are $1.25 a day or more for hired labor on ranches. . . . Men are generally called by their Christian names (or given names, as they say out here). The laborer who is hired is generally on the same social footing as his boss—works with him and has meals with him. The term 'servant' is not in use in the county districts. . . . It is quite the right things to go to any ranch and demand a meal, and you are expected to offer 50 cents for it on leaving, though they generally will not take anything. If you are 'broke' you can nearly always get a meal, etc., either free or in exchange for a little work, e.g. chopping wood. Most of the people have been "broke" some time or other, so they can sympathize with those who are in this condition better than they otherwise would. Butter and eggs can be sold in town or to neighboring ranches, similarly potatoes, etc. Hay and oats are also sold as well as grown for consumption on the ranch. Horse-trading is profitable to those who know about horses. It is held no disgrace to cheat in a horse trade, and friends will so cheat one another. Cattle may be sold alive, or as meat. Pigs are rather a good investment.

It was in this environment that the Beckwiths were poised to prosper.

CHAPTER 13

Senator Elton T. Beckwith

As the Beckwith Brothers' fortune continued to grow, they expanded their ranches and began investing in mining and other ventures around the valley and the state. The brothers joined the Republican Party in addition to helping form the Wet Mountain Valley Cattlemen's Association.

The Republican Party in 1884 was the "Party of Lincoln" and on June 3, 1884, it assembled at the Republican National Convention to announce its party platform. This platform included the following:

The Republican party has, after saving the Union, done so much to render its institutions just, equal and beneficent, the safeguard of liberty and the embodiment of the best thought and highest purpose of our citizens.

The Republican party has gained its strength by quick and faithful response to the demands of the people for the freedom and equality of all men; for the elevation of labor, for an honest currency; for purity in legislation, and for integrity and accountability in all departments of the government, and it accepts anew the duty of leading in the work of progress and reform.

Elton and Edwin Beckwith supported these concepts and actively promoted them. Elton's obituary in the June 1, 1907,

Figure 33: Elton Beckwith, later in life
Courtesy of History Colorado, Accession 2000.129.346

Wet Mountain Tribune stated, "Mr. Beckwith was a stalwart Republican, nor ever could his position on questions of national or state import be mistaken."

Other planks in the 1884 Republican platform included:

- A free ballot, an honest count, and correct returns
- Lower taxes
- Public regulation of railway corporations to prevent unjust discrimination and excessive charges for transportation
- The establishment of a national bureau of labor and enforcement of the eight hour law
- A wise and judicious system of general education by adequate appropriation from the national revenues [free general education]

In 1886, Elton Beckwith was elected a Colorado senator on the Republican ticket. While serving, he was a member of the Committee on Education. Elton purchased a mansion at 1900 East Fourteenth Street on Capitol Hill, and he, Elsie, and Velma moved to Denver. There they met many wealthy and influential people.

Elton served only one two-year term and then they moved back to Waverly Ranch in the Wet Mountain Valley. He continued to make additions to the ranch. The family also traveled around the world, just as Edwin had been doing. They visited Persia, Egypt, Asia, and New Mexico. Elsie and Velma purchased exotic items to decorate the mansion and guest houses. They created theme guest rooms: the Persian Room, Native American Room, and Oriental Room.

The town of Westcliffe was founded in 1881 when the Denver & Rio Grande Railroad brought its narrow-gauge line up Grape Creek from Cañon City. Ignoring Silver Cliff, the

**Figure 34: The Native American Room at the
Beckwith Ranch, circa 1900**
Courtesy of History Colorado, Accession #98.273.15
Photographed by Eugenia Ransom Kennicott

narrow-gauge branch terminated on land owned by William
Bell. Bell originally established the town of Clifton for the
terminus but later named it Westcliffe, incorporating it in
1887. As the railway terminal, Westcliffe became the main
hub for the Wet Mountain Valley's farming and ranching
community.

The Rocky Mountain News reported that the first passenger
train arrived on May 11, 1881. Excursion trains, bringing tourists into the valley, were very popular, but freight cars were
needed to carry minerals, cattle, and produce out of Custer
County to market and were the primary justification for the

**Figure 35: The Oriental Room at the
Beckwith Ranch, circa 1900**
Courtesy of History Colorado, Accession #98.273.16
Photographed by Eugenia Ransom Kennicott

railway. In the summer, vegetables, peas, lettuce, and cabbage were shipped out. In the fall, cattle filled the railway cars. It was not unusual for cattle cars to extend for a quarter mile.

Grape Creek floods wiped out the tracks three times in the first nine years, causing the Denver & Rio Grande to stop its Silver Cliff line. Ten years later the railroad returned, using a drier route farther west that followed Texas Creek up through the Wet Mountain Valley. This new railroad crossed the Waverly Ranch and operated until 1938. An engineering feat called the Lariat Loop enabled the train to gain the altitude needed to reach the Wet Mountain Valley. The track loops like

Figure 36: Train wreck after a flood on Grape Creek, 1885

Courtesy of the Old Westcliffe Schoolhouse Collection

a lariat when viewed from above. The loop is set at a steady incline as it circles higher. The Lariat Loop was constructed at the Texas Creek station at the Arkansas River.

According to a contract in the Beckwith Ranch archives, the Denver & Rio Grande Railway paid Elton Beckwith $1,600 for the right to cross his ranch. He also received his own whistle-stop, called Verdemont, as part of the deal. In the fall, the Beckwiths and neighboring ranchers could load their cattle at the whistle-stop for shipments to markets back east. However, most ranchers drove their cattle to the stockyards in Westcliffe to be loaded.

Elsie found the whistle-stop particularly useful for her visitors coming mostly from Denver, but also from Colorado Springs, Cañon City and Pueblo. Elsie had carriages waiting to transport them from the whistle-stop to Waverly Ranch

Figure 37: The Lariat Loop as seen from Inspiration Point
Courtesy of the Beckwith Ranch Collection
Photograph by M. Lowe

where she greeted them as they unloaded under the *porte cochère,* which had been built just for this purpose.

Life was good for the Beckwiths. The ranch grew to eighty-eight hundred acres. At its peak, the Beckwiths were reported to have around two hundred horses and seven thousand head of cattle. It was one of the largest and most successful cattle operations in Colorado.

A revealing story has been handed down from this time. It is said that Elton and Edwin told Elsie they were going to Westcliffe on business. Elsie was not fooled, knowing they were really headed for Dutch Row, a wild part of Westcliffe along Second Street. Dutch Row was where the beer joints, bars, boardinghouses, and brothels were located.

According to the story, Elsie was furious; her temper growing as the evening passed and it got later and later. She loaded a shotgun and waited in the ballroom for Elton's return. When Elton staggered in late that night and passed from the entry way to the ballroom, Elsie pointed the shotgun in his face and shouted, "That's the last time you're going to Dutch Row!"

Elton slapped the barrel with his hand, spinning Elsie around, and the gun discharged, shooting the southwest corner floor of the ballroom. It is uncertain how much of this story is true, but there remains to this day scars in the southwest corner of the ballroom from a shotgun blast.

Farming in the Wet Mountain Valley virtually ended after railroad service was terminated in 1938. One by one, many of the other towns in Custer County faded, leaving Westcliffe to become a trading center and resort area.

Figure 38: Beckwith Ranch and its private whistle-stop
Courtesy of the Matt Richter Collection

CHAPTER 14

The Downfall of the Dynasty

I f 1870 was the turning point for the Beckwiths, when the whole family looked west, left behind their businesses, or started new careers that led to great fortune and fame, 1892 was the turning point for when it all began to unravel.

The matriarch of the Beckwith family, Tamesin Heath Beckwith, did not live to see the great successes of her husband and sons. She passed away shortly after the 1870 turning point. She died in 1873 and was buried in Riverside Cemetery in Denver.

George Beckwith carried on after Tamesin's death, initially helping his sons by forming the Beckwith & Sons Cattle Investment Company and later helping them build the Beckwith Brothers Cattle Ranch. He also bought his own ranch in the Longmont area near Denver.

In 1875, George married Mary Rosa Hair, but she passed away within a few years of their marriage. Then, in 1880, he married Anna Grace Seaton. Anna Grace was a Denver social-ite. The *Rocky Mountain News* wrote about their marriage on February 3, 1880:

> The NEWS is pleased to record the marriage of Mr. George C. Beckwith, one of Denver's prominent capitalists, to Miss Grace, only daughter of Mrs. J. K. Seaton. The difference between sixty-five and eighteen is bridged to the entire satisfaction of the contracting parties, who started on their wedding tour to Salt Lake city and the Pacific coast by yesterday morning's express.

In 1885, George and Grace moved to Oakland, California and Grace gave birth to their son, George Chipman II. George I, the patriarch of the Beckwith family, died on April 19, 1892, after a short illness which was described in his death certificate as "calculous Nephralgia," a kidney condition. His body was escorted home to Denver by his widow, Grace, and six-year-old George II. He was buried in Riverside Cemetery next to his first wife, Tamesin.

His obituary in the April 19, 1892, *Rocky Mountain News* reads:

> George C. Beckwith who was one of the best known capitalists of Denver died in Oakland, California April 19, after a short illness. The body arrived here last night in charge of the widow of the deceased, Mrs. Grace Beckwith. Elton T. Beckwith and Edwin F. Beckwith, of Westcliffe, George, a six year old son was also in the party. The funeral will take place this afternoon at 2 o'clock, from Rogers undertaking rooms at Riverside, where the remains will be interred.

Polly Chapin, Elsie's mother, died just a few months before George, at the end of 1891, and was buried in the Ula Cemetery two miles from Waverly Ranch. Her obituary was posted in the *Silver Cliff Rustler* on December 30, 1891:

Died: At the residence of her daughter, Mrs. E. T. Beckwith, in Wet Mountain Valley, on the morning of Dec. 27th., Mrs. P. R. Chapin, aged 76 years. The funeral services were held at the residence of Senator and Mrs. Beckwith on Monday, Dec. 28th and was attended by a large concourse of friends. Mrs. Chapin was a most estimable lady, beloved by everyone who knew her. No words can do justice to her excellent qualities. She was a perfect christian lady. The sincere sympathies of the entire community as felt for the bereaved relatives are joined in by the Rustler.

The survivors carried on, but in 1898 more troubles arose.

Elton and Elsie's daughter, Velma, grew up as a cowgirl, living the ranching life. She was a favorite of her uncle Edwin. In 1897, when Velma was around eighteen, Elsie and Elton decided to move back into their Denver mansion so that Velma would have a chance to meet wealthy, powerful, and eligible bachelors. They threw lavish parties to try to ensure that Velma would marry well.

Unfortunately, she somehow met and fell in love with an assay clerk, Norris Wilcox. An assay clerk is a low-level chemist who weighs and checks the purity of ores and minerals, such as gold and silver, in an assay office. Wilcox was handsome and outgoing, but he was an orphan and therefore not from a wealthy or powerful family. In addition, he was reputed to be a Catholic, not an Episcopalian. These virtues were so far below Elsie Beckwith's vision for her daughter that she found the relationship to be embarrassing and even scandalous. Elsie forbade her daughter from seeing Wilcox ever again.

Defiantly, on August 14, 1898, Velma eloped and married Wilcox in the nearby town of Littleton, Colorado. The family was shocked, embarrassed, and humiliated. Elton and Elsie disowned their only child. According to an article in the *Rocky Mountain News,* published on November 27, 1898, "Miss Velma proudly asserted that she would marry the man she loved, whether the choice met with her parental opposition or approval." Therefore Elton "declared that he had absolutely disinherited his daughter, and that she would get nothing when he died; the uncle has carried out his determination, too, for his will, filed yesterday, does not even mention the name of his niece."

Just before Velma's marriage, Edwin returned from a trip to Japan and fell ill with Bright's disease. Bright's disease is an inflammation of the kidneys caused by toxins, infection, or autoimmune conditions. Edwin was staying in the Brown Palace Hotel and was so ashamed of Velma that he wouldn't allow her to visit him. Velma never saw him alive again. Edwin passed away on November 13, 1898, leaving his entire estate to his brother. But his obituary reported that with his final breath, he called for "the niece I love better than life itself."

Elton and Elsie felt so disgraced by Velma's elopement that they sold the mansion in Denver and moved back to Waverly Ranch, transferring much of the furniture with the move back. Feeling their reputation was tarnished, they spent the next several years trying to rebuild their status and reputation.

After Edwin died, Elton moved his brother's ranch house to Waverly Ranch near the guest cottages. It most likely served as additional guest quarters after that, but it was surely a curiosity to show to friends and visitors. The November 5, 1892, *Herald Democrat* described Edwin's home:

> About three miles from Ula is his ranch house, a bungalow painted white, with sixteen foot verandas on all sides. The bungalow is fitted as no other house in existence, the only thing American being a range and a bathroom. For the last decade Mr. Beckwith has employed his winters traveling in faroff lands and picking up curios and articles of vertu. These have been shipped home, and as a result his house looks more like a museum than anything else. Although a bachelor, Mr. Beckwith is a sybarite, and the incongruity of an Egyptian mummy leering under an electric light rather amuses him. Be it known that no woman, save his sister-in-law has ever set foot in the charming place he calls "the ranch."

To recover from the disgrace of Velma's marriage, Elsie sought to bring Waverly Ranch up to lofty standards that would properly impress their wealthy friends. By 1903, they had added the larder on the north side of the house. A gazebo and fountain were built in front of the mansion, complete with walkways and flower gardens. Elton added calving barns behind his workshop and built a grand water tower near the road with a pump house underneath. Waverly Ranch was the first in the valley to have running water and electricity. It was the second to have a telephone; the phone number was Silver 142.

Figure 39: The Beckwith Ranch circa 1903. Note the gazebo, fountain, and Edwin's house on the far left.

Courtesy of the Beckwith Ranch Collection

Elton and Elsie continued to travel the world, purchasing items to decorate the mansion and guest houses. Newspaper articles describing their lifestyle and home indicate that by 1903 they had successfully accomplished their goal of reestablishing their status in Colorado.

Unfortunately, Velma had made a terrible mistake with her marriage. Wilcox was abusive. In their divorce papers, Norris Wilcox was charged with, and found guilty of, extreme and repeated acts of cruelty. The divorce was awarded, and he was ordered to pay $200 and $75 per month until Velma remarried.

The following excerpts from an article in the *Cañon City Record*, printed on June 14, 1906, reveal Velma's strained relationship with her parents until her divorce:

> The reconciliation with [Velma's] parents was delayed through all those years. The Wilcoxes had been married a number of years, when one night they dined at the Brown Palace hotel, accidentally at the table next to the mother and father of the daughter. Acting upon the advice of his wife, Mr. Wilcox walked over to Mr. Beckwith and extended his hand. He was met with a stare and a quote "I don't know you, sir." This incident ended all attempts to patch up the differences between daughter and parents until Mr. and Mrs. Beckwith learned in the past two months that their daughter contemplated suing for an absolute divorce. Then they forgave her and wanted her to return to the parental roof.

After her divorce, Velma moved back home to Waverly Ranch. Her parents welcomed her home but, the relationship was probably strained since she spent much of the next few years traveling and visiting friends. By the end of 1906, Elton developed paresis, a brain disorder that caused him to hallucinate, become irrational, and develop paralysis and blindness. Paresis is a result of prolonged syphilis. As his illness progressed, it appears that Elton grew close to his wayward daughter. He was incapable of changing his will but instructed Elsie that Velma receive half of the estate when he died.

Elsie hired nurses to look after Elton and moved him into the upstairs corridor between her bedroom and Velma's bedroom. She tried to confine him there.

In 1907, Elton's condition worsened. The prognosis was not good. Elsie knew that she and Velma could no longer manage the ranch, and she, at least, had no desire to continue to live there. She had an attorney and physician declare Elton incompetent. In an article titled "Wife Appointed to Care for Estate of Husband," the *Rocky Mountain News* reported on May 25, 1907:

Canon City, Colo., May 24.—Mrs. Elsie A. Beckwith, wife of ex-Senator Elton Beckwith of Hillside, has been appointed conservatrix of her husband's estate. The ex-senator has been suffering from paresis for months and now is constantly confined to his bed. He has been one of the most prominent figures in Custer county for thirty-seven years. The appointment was made necessary in order that title could be given to the stock ranch and homestead, which were sold to Baker and Biggs a week ago for $70,000.

Elsie sold Waverly Ranch to Baker and Biggs Realty of Cañon City with the stipulation that she and her daughter could continue to live on the ranch until Elton passed away. According to the May 22, 1907, edition of the *Silver Cliff*

Rustler, the sale included "the home place and several hundred acres of additional pasture and grazing land. About 2,700 head of cattle, fifty head of registered Hereford stock, including the second prize Herford bull at the St. Louis fair and some 200 head of horses."

Only a few days after closing on the sale of the ranch, on May 26, 1907, around noon, Elton fell from a second-story window at the ranch. On June 13, 1907, the *Cañon City Record* wrote a detailed description of Elton's fall and death:

Mr. Beckwith had for months been a sufferer from paresis, and eventually would have died of that disease, but his death was hastened by injuries received last Tuesday, when he evaded his nurse and jumped from a second-story window. The fall was responsible for several fractures, and it is believed that internal injuries were also received.

News of the death of Mr. Beckwith was withheld until Saturday from his only child, Mrs. Elsie Velma Wilcox, because of Mrs. Wilcox's nervous condition. She had been visiting friends in eastern cities for several weeks and was notified in Chicago his injuries would probably prove fatal. She started for Denver, arriving Friday morning, a few hours after her father had died.

The journey took much of her strength, and on her arrival in Denver she was in a condition bordering on total collapse. To make matters worse came an order of court to give a deposition in the Helen A. Low case in the district court. It was in opposition to her physician's orders that she gave her testimony to attorneys Friday evening.

Friends who have known the young woman from the time she was a lassie in short skirts, remained with her Friday, Friday night, all day Saturday and Saturday night.

It was finally decided to break the news to her late Saturday afternoon. . . .

The way in which Elton T. Beckwith died was a sad ending to a career of brilliance. Intimate friends had known for six weeks that the end was not far distant. Mr. Beckwith had been confined to a room at his Wet Mountain country home for several months, guarded night and day by nurses who never for a minute left him. Two months ago he began to grow violent.

The day of his escape from the nurses and his fall from the second-story window, it was decided to remove him to Dr. Work's sanitarium in Pueblo.

It was necessary to use force in controlling him on the trip to Pueblo. Sheriff Hendershot of Pueblo and two deputies, with Dr. Baldwin, the Beckwith family physician, and other assistants, acted as escort.

Experts were summoned from Denver and the plan was to secure the best medical talent in Chicago and New York to consult in the case. But Dr. Baldwin and other physicians informed relatives and friends that there was no earthly power to extend the patient's life.

The only thing to do, they said, and the only thing that could be done, was to sit calmly by and wait for death, which could not be far away. When death finally took the patient by the hand, there was no sign of violence; sleep had come and death simply pushed away sleep without disturbing the sufferer.

Elton's obituary in the *Wet Mountain Valley Tribune*, the local Westcliffe newspaper, posted on June 1, 1907, states:

This morning flashed the sad news from Pueblo of the death of Elton T. Beckwith, one of Custer County's most prominent and highly respected citizens, which occurred at Work's Sanitarium to which he had been removed the first of this week, between two and three o'clock this morning. Mrs. Beckwith and daughter were at his bedside when the end came.

Deceased was born on Mount Desert Island on the coast of Maine April 1st, 1847, 60 years, 2 months and 8 days ago; was educated in the schools of Cambridge and Boston. In 1869, he came to Denver from Philadelphia, at which latter place he had for three years previous having been engaged in mercantile business, his brother, the late Edwin F. having located in Wet Mountain valley the year previous. A partnership was entered into by the two brothers and only a few years elapsed ere they were recognized as the heaviest stock growers in the State, which proved immensely profitable to both.

In 1875 Mr. Beckwith married the widow of Charles Davis, a brother of the late J. A. Davis, who survives him. But one child was born to them, Mrs. Velma Wilcox, of Denver.

Mr. Beckwith was a stalwart Republican, nor ever could his position on questions of national or state import be mistaken. He served his party in the state senate as a member from this county and could, had he desired it, been returned. At one time he was somewhat prominently spoken of for governor. He was honorable in all his dealings and in his passing Custer County has lost one of her staunchest and best citizens.

The remains will be brought from Pueblo to Waverly, his late home, from whence they will be taken to the family burial grounds in Ula cemetery for interment on Monday.

Elsie and Velma vacated Waverly Ranch soon after Elton's

death. Elsie moved into the exclusive Brown Palace Hotel, purchased Velma a "modest" house in Denver, and gave her $83.33 per month to live on. After a few years, Elsie purchased a nice home near where she and Elton had lived before in Denver, on 1421 Gilpin Street in the wealthy neighborhood of Capitol Hill. She would live there until her death from pneumonia in 1931.

Velma was expecting her mother to split the family estate. She had heard her father tell Elsie it was his wish, but Elsie never followed up on his request. Velma married Homer Allen Lentz on May 2, 1914.

Although she was a multi-millionaire in 1907, Elsie's fortunes would not last. Much of her wealth was spent on attorneys trying to settle the Beckwith brothers' complex estate. When Elsie died, her 1928 will had the following behests:

- $5,000 to daughter, Velma Lentz;
- The proceeds from securities to be given to brother Rufus Chapin;
- $1,000 to Mrs. Renetta Van Schaack;
- $4,000 to Charles Burkhardt;
- $6,500 to cousin Denver R. Pratt plus her square dinner ring containing eighteen diamonds;
- To Sarah Burkhardt her pear-shaped solitaire ring with diamond setting;
- $100 to John Clare;
- $500 to Mrs. Esther Mallow;
- $100 to Evalyn Laurentz;
- $100 to Martha Laurentz;
- $200 to Eugenia Kennicott;
- and $200 to Rose Bouregard.

- The remainder was to go to Denver R. Platt and Charles A. Burkhardt, executors of the estate.

The stock market crash of 1929 wiped out her securities, but by then, her brother Rufus had passed away. Elsie had wished to be buried in Denver, but when she died on August 17, 1931, the executors decided she did not have the finances to afford a plot in Denver, so her remains were returned to the Wet Mountain Valley accompanied by cousin, Denver Pratt. She was buried next to Elton in the Beckwith plot in the Ula Cemetery.

Probate reveals that at this point, after selling all her assets, her net worth was $21,130. Her will doled out $17,700 leaving only $3,430. The executors, by burying her in the Wet Mountain Valley against her wishes, received more of the remaining balance.

Velma had married Homer Allen Lentz, an engineer, and the couple had moved to Chicago. It appears to have been a happy marriage until Homer died in 1927. Velma then moved to Los Angeles, California, to be with friends.

It is believed that after her tragic and violent marriage to Norris Wilcox, Velma suffered from ill health for the rest of her life. Excerpts from the following letter to Gerald Hughes, an old friend, dated September 1, 1931, exposes the loneliness and poor condition of Velma at the end:

My mother has recently passed on and, as I am utterly alone here in Los Angeles, I am harking back to old friendship to ask if you would look into certain matters should they require investigation.

I have been a semi-invalid for the past four years and forbidden to go to Colorado on account of my heart.

As I have not received my copy of Mother's will, and

the only information I have to date is from a personal letter from a friend.

After receiving a favorable letter from Hughes, Velma wrote a second letter to him, dated September 11, 1931:

It is difficult for me to express my appreciation of your kindness, especially in my present predicament. My eyes having given out, together with further troubles (alone and without sufficient funds to employ help) I did not know to whom to turn when this latest shock came to me. . . .

The eye specialist states that I shall be fortunate if my eyes do not become any worse. . . . Dr. Bailey, my physician . . . has forbidden me absolutely to go to Colorado, on account of my heart trouble. . . .

The agreement to which you refer was one giving me $1,000 per year for life, which I signed at my Mother's request, after consenting not to break my Father's will; he left everything to Mother when she promised to divide the estate half and half with me. She of course agreed to see that I received more than the $83.03 per month, however, after coming to California and not wishing to deprive her of any luxuries in her old age, also not wishing to worry her with my troubles, I have been living on that amount in cheap boarding houses. At present, I am living with friends, and am practically without funds until some settlement is made in the matter.

I merely mention these facts so that you may judge whether or not I am within my rights in questioning the fairness of this distribution of our estate.

Velma passed away three months later, on December 23,

1931, only a few months after her mother's death. In October 1933, a petition to force the executors Denver R Platt and Charles A. Burkhardt, to pay Velma $5,000 finally made it to court, two years after Velma passed away.

Probate for Velma's will showed that she was completely broke. She never had any children and was buried in Inglewood, California. The death of Elsie and Velma marked the tragic end of the Beckwith's from the Wet Mountain Valley.

George Chipman Beckwith started out with very little when he moved to New York from Nova Scotia, Canada. He worked hard and saved enough to establish himself as a merchant and shipbuilder on Mount Desert Island, Maine. He saw to it that his family was always comfortable financially. His sons Elton and Edwin built on his investment and became fabulously wealthy, only to lose it all in the end.

Still, the ranch they built lived on, changing hands many times before being purchased by Paul Seegers ninety years later.

CHAPTER 16

The Beckwith Ranch Lives On

The Beckwith Ranch lived on for a while, but times change. Elsie Beckwith sold the ranch to Baker and Biggs Realty of Cañon City on May 22, 1907. Baker and Briggs sold it to George A. Starbird on October 9, 1907. Starbird bought both the ranch and the Beckwiths' Lazy T cattle brand.

Starbird sold the ranch on June 23, 1911, to A. K. Marselus, who sold it to the Overfelt family on October 22, 1920. The Overfelts added several barns to the headquarters. It was still known as the Waverly Ranch when they sold it in 1929 to William MacKenzie. The Overfelts are thought to be the last owners to live in the Beckwith Ranch mansion.

William MacKenzie owned a number of ranches and lived in Cañon City. He paid $27,500 for Waverly Ranch in 1929 and expanded it from eighty-eight hundred acres to thirteen thousand. On July 3, 1946, MacKenzie sold Waverly Ranch to Mac Clevenger, a wealthy car dealer from Pueblo. From then until 1996, it was known as the Clevenger Ranch. Clevenger expanded the ranch to thirty-three thousand acres, buying all the land from Waverly Ranch north to the Arkansas River so that he could drive cattle on his own land all the way to the railroad stockyards at Texas Creek. Clevenger made many changes to the Beckwith mansion, including covering the siding with stucco, upgrading the kitchen, and adding an indoor first-floor bathroom. Although he never lived in the mansion, his ranch foreman and later ranch families occupied it through the 1980s.

After Clevenger passed away, his widow sold the ranch in

Figure 40: Christmas card showing the Beckwith Ranch, circa 1925

Courtesy of the Beckwith Ranch Collection

Figure 41: Beckwith Ranch, circa 1908
Courtesy of the Beckwith Ranch Collection

1982 to Roland Walters from Kerrville, Texas. Walters converted much of the ranch into the Bull Domingo and Cody Park housing developments. Walters also owned the famed Wolf Springs Ranch in the southern portion of the valley.

In 1992, Paul Seegers traded his three-thousand-acre Circle S Ranch in Texas for the eighty-eight hundred acres that made up the original Waverly Ranch. The mansion and surrounding buildings were crumbling, rotting, and sinking into the marshy land. Seegers considered donating the buildings to the Westcliffe Fire Department so the firefighters could practice fire rescue there, but his wife, Phyllis, and a good friend, Linda Kaufman, wanted to save and restore the ranch. Encouraged by his daughter, Pam, and son-in-law, Jon Gaulding, Seegers set aside 3.85 acres containing the remaining ranch buildings. He was willing to lease the land and structures provided that Phyllis and Linda could acquire grants and money for the restoration.

They formed the 501(c)(3) non-profit organization, Friends of Beckwith Ranch, Inc. in 1996. The new non-profit leased the 3.85 acres from Seegers for ninety-nine years for one dollar. They then listed all ten of the buildings on the National Register of Historic Places.

The Seegers would later sell the ranch to Bill and Suzanne "Smokey" Jack with the stipulation that the 3.85 acres would go to Friends of Beckwith Ranch, Inc. once a variance from the county was approved. The 3.85 acres received the variance, and Bill Jack signed over the buildings and acreage to the Friends of Beckwith Ranch in 1998. After Smokey passed away, Bill moved to California and left the ranch to Smokey's daughter. She kept the ranch until 2021 and sold it to cattle ranchers Tate and Wendy Rusk.

Friends of the Beckwith Ranch now owned the property and restoration could begin. Over the past twenty-five years, Friends of the Beckwith Ranch has worked tirelessly to repair, restore, and maintain the old ranch, but all that hard work is a story for another book.

Beckwith Dynasty Timeline

1817 **July 24, 1817**, George Chipman Beckwith born

1823 **March 9, 1823**, Tamesin F. Heath Beckwith born

1844 George C. Beckwith becomes a naturalized U.S. citizen and marries Tamisin F. Heath

1845 **December 6, 1845,** Elsie Chapin Davis Beckwith born

1845 **February 12, 1845,** Loring Everett Beckwith born

1847 **April 1, 1847**, Elton Towers Beckwith born

1849 **April 4, 1849**, Edwin F. Beckwith born

1850 US census shows George Beckwith and family living in Ellsworth, Maine

1860 US census shows George Beckwith and family living in Cambridge, Massachusetts

1863 Elton Beckwith attends Comer's Commercial College

1865 Loring Beckwith graduates from Harvard College

Elton Beckwith graduates from Comer's Commercial College and starts a flour, feed, and grain business in Philadelphia

Edwin Beckwith attends Comer's Commercial College

1869 Edwin and George Beckwith travel to the Colorado Territory. Edwin settles on land in the Wet Mountain Valley

1870 Loring Beckwith graduates from Harvard Divinity School

US census shows George Chipman and family (without older sons) living in Denver City

October 15, 1870, Elton Beckwith moves to the Wet Mountain Valley

1871 **April 28, 1871**, Loring Beckwith marries Alice Campbell Houghton Beckwith

September 7, 1871, Elsie A. Chapin marries Charles Davis

1872 Charles Davis dies and leaves their ranch, the Half Circle D, to Elsie.

1873 **July 2, 1873**, Loring Beckwith is ordained as a paster for the Church of Christ, in Augusta, Maine

November 1, 1873, Tamesin F. Beckwith dies

1875 **February 8, 1875**, Elton Beckwith marries Elsie Davis, adding the Half Circle D Ranch to the Beckwith Ranch

August 4, 1875, George Beckwith marries Mary Rosa Hair

1878 Edwin Beckwith represents Custer County at the Republican State Convection

1879 Elsie Velma Beckwith is born to Elton and Elsie

Edwin Beckwith is on the Committee of Credentials at the Custer County Republican Convention

1880   **February 3, 1880**, George Beckwith marries Anna Grace Seaton

1885   George and Anna Beckwith move to Oakland, California

1886   Elton Beckwith is elected a Colorado state senator

1889   **December 10, 1889**, Edwin Beckwith applies for a US passport

       Willie Hendrickson, a broncobuster, goes to work at Beckwith Ranch

1891   **December 30, 1891,** Polly Chapin dies and is buried in Ula Cemetery

1892   **April 19, 1892**, George Beckwith dies

1897   Elton Beckwith and family move to Denver to introduce Velma to proper society

1895   Loring Beckwith dies

1898   **September 14, 1898**, Velma Beckwith elopes with Norris Wilcox

       November 13, 1898, Edwin Beckwith dies

1900   **January 26, 1900**, Elton Beckwith applies for a US passport for himself and his wife, Elsie Beckwith

1901   Elton and Elsie Beckwith travel to Europe, the Cuban islands, and the Philippines

1906   **June 10, 1906**, Velma Beckwith Wilcox divorces Norris Wilcox

1907   **May 22, 1907**, Elsie Beckwith agrees to sell Beckwith Ranch to Baker and Biggs Realty

June 1, 1907, Elton Beckwith dies. Elsie and Velma move to the Brown Palace in Denver

October 9, 1907, Baker and Biggs sells Beckwith Ranch to George A. Starbird

1909   Else Beckwith purchases a mansion at 1421 Gilpin

1911   **June 23, 1911**, George A. Starbird sells Beckwith Ranch to A. K. Marselus

1914   **May 2, 1914**, Velma Beckwith marries Homer Lentz

1920   **October 22, 1920**, A. K. Marselus sells Beckwith Ranch to the Overfelt family

1929   The Overfelts sell Beckwith Ranch to William MacKenzie

1931   **August 17, 1931**, Elsie Beckwith dies in Denver

1931   **December 23, 1931**, Velma Beckwith dies

1946   **July 3, 1946**, William MacKenzie sells Beckwith Ranch to Mac Clevenger

1982   Mac Clevenger dies and his widow sells Beckwith Ranch to Roland Walters

1992   Paul and Phyllis Seegers trade their Circle S Ranch for the Beckwith Ranch

1996   Seegers begin the process of donating Beckwith Ranch to the nonprofit group Friends of Beckwith Ranch

1996   Friends of Beckwith Ranch sign a ninety-nine-year lease on the Ranch

Bibliography

Books and Articles

American Presidency Project. "Republican Party Platform of 1884." 2024. https://www.presidency.ucsb.edu/documents/republican-party-platform-1884.

Anderson, Wayne I. "The Historic Mines of Custer County, Colorado." Sangre de Cristo Natural History. 2006. https://sites.uni.edu/andersow/historicmines.html.

Bar Harbor Times. "Sailing a Business Enterprise Not an Adventure to Sailors of Eden." May 6, 1965.

Beckwith, Paul. *The Beckwiths.* Albany: Joel Munsell's Sons, 1991.

Binckley & Hartwell, comp. *Southern Colorado.* Cañon City, CO: Rand, McNally, 1879.

Boulder County Pioneer. "Sheriff's Sale." June 2, 1869.

Buffington-Sammons, Judy. "Cattle Rustling and Quick Justice." *Fence Post.* March 19, 2007. https://www.thefencepost.com/news/cattle-rustling-and-quick-justice/.

Campbell, Rosemae Wells. *From Trappers to Tourists: Fremont County 1830–1950.* Cañon City, CO: Fremont-Custer Historical Society, 1972.

Cañon City Record. May 23, 1901.

——. "Cuts Off Daughter without a Cent." June 20, 1907.

——. "Laid to Rest." November 17, 1898.

——. "Senator E. T. Beckwith of Custer County Died in Pueblo Sanitarium." June 13, 1907.

——. "Well Known Girl Divorces Husband." June 14, 1906.

Carrillo, Richard F., and Daniel A. Jepson. *A Study in Historical Archaeology at the Tremont House Hotel, Lower Downtown Denver.* Denver: Colorado Department of Transportation and the Federal Highway Administration, 1995. https://archaeologycolorado.org/sites/default/files/Carrillo%20and%20Jepson%201995%20Tremont%20House.pdf.

Catalogue of the Trustees, Officers, Teachers, and Students of Washington Academy 1860. East Machias, ME: Washington Academy.

Chicago Tribune. "Married." September 8, 1871.

Cockerell, Theodore D. A. *Theodore D. A. Cockerell: Letters from West Cliff, Colorado, 1887–1889.* Boulder: Colorado Associated University Press, 1976.

Colorado Daily Chieftain (Pueblo). June 2, 1873.

———."Custer County Republican Convention." September 18, 1879.

Colorado Springs Pioneers Museum. "Dr. William A. Bell." 2024. https://www.cspm.org/cos-150-story/dr-william-a-bell/.

Colorado Weekly Chieftain (Pueblo). February 24, 1870.

———."4,000 Head of Cattle." November 10, 1870.

———."Republican State Convention." August 8, 1878.

———"A Romantic Ride over the Greenhorn Range." November 13, 1872.

Cross, Coy F. *Go West, Young Man! Horace Greeley's Vision for America.* Albuquerque: University of New Mexico Press, 1995.

Custer County Cattle Growers' Association. *Brand Book.* Westcliffe, CO: Wet Mountain Tribune, 1899.

Custer County Past and Present: A Historical Digest for Exploring the Wet Mountain Valley. Westcliffe, CO: Custer County Tourism, 2023.

Daily Herald (Silver Cliff, CO). July 21, 1882.

Daily Tribune (Florence, CO). "Old Beckwith Ranch Purchased in Valley." March 12, 1929.

Denver Times. "Homes in the Hills." October 13, 1901.

Dodds, Joanne West. *Custer County: Rosita, Silver Cliff, and*

Westcliffe. Pueblo: Focal Plain, 1994.

Ellsworth American (Ellsworth, ME). July 17, 1857.

——."New Store! New Goods! New Firm!" October 9, 1857.

Genealogy Trails, History Group. "History of Custer County." 2024. https://genealogytrails.com/colo/custer/history.html.

Goodnight Barn Historic Preservation Committee. "About Charles Goodnight." 2021. https://www.goodnightbarn-pueblo.org/about.

Harper's Weekly Journal of Civilization. "A Colorado Colony." March 26, 1870. https://archive.org/details/harpersweek-lyv14bonn/page/196/mode/2up.

Herald Democrat (Leadville). "Story of an Old Frontier Feud." November 5, 1892.

History Colorado. "Gervacio Nolan Land Grant Original Documents." 2024. https://www.historycolorado.org/node/55458.

History of the Arkansas Valley, Colorado. Chicago: O. L. Baskin, 1881. https://upload.wikimedia.org/wikipedia/commons/6/65/History_of_the_Arkansas_Valley,_Colorado_(IA_cu31924028878754).pdf.

Holley, John Stokes. *The Invisible People of the Pikes Peak Region.* Colorado Springs: Friends of the Colorado Springs Pioneers Museum, 1990.

Hughes, Jim. *Living in Custer County: A Rural Colorado Lifestyle* Bloomington, IN: Abbott Press, 2011.

Kennicott, Anna. *"Learn to Labor and Wait:" The 1899 Diary of Anna Kennicott, age 11.* Westcliffe, CO: Crestone Graphics, 1993.

Lake County Star (Baldwin, MI). "Gold Phantoms: Fascinating Tales of Lost Mines." November 25, 1938.

Lake County Tourism Panel. "Native American History in Leadville and Twin Lakes." November 19, 2021. https://www.leadvilletwinlakes.com/blog-article/native-american-history-in-leadville-and-twin-lakes/.

Legislative, Historical and Biographical Compendium of Colorado.

Denver: C. F. Coleman's Publishing House, 1887.
https://archive.org/details/legislativehisto00cfcorich.

Miller, Victor W. "The McCoy Gang." *Old West.* Summer 1970.

Mount Desert 365. "Mount Desert's Maritime Past, Present, and Future." 2024. https://mountdesert365.org/mount-deserts-maritime-past-present-and-future/

Noel, Thomas J. *Riding High: Colorado Ranchers and 100 Years of the National Western Stock Show.* Arvada, CO: Fulcrum Publishing, 2005.

Olson, Lee. *Marmalade and Whiskey: British Remittance Men in the West.* Arvada, CO: Fulcrum Publishing, 1993.

Portrait and Biographical Record of Denver and Vicinity, Colorado. Chicago: Chapman Publishing Company, 1898. https://ia600304.us.archive.org/5/items/biographportrait00chaprich/biographportrait00chaprich.pdf.

Pueblo Star-Journal and Sunday Chieftain. "Historic Beckwith Ranch Graces Wet Mountain Valley." September 5, 1954.

Risk, Shannon M. "Biographical Sketch of Alice Campbell Houghton Beckwith." Alexander Street. 2024. https://documents.alexanderstreet.com/d/1011002123.

Rocky Mountain News (Denver). April 26, 1870; February 28, 1897; July 30, 1899; May 30, 1872; October 25, 1871.

———."Arrivals and Departures." June 15, 1869; August 3, 1869; October 25, 1869; October 26, 1869; October 30, 1869; November 3, 1869; December 10, 1869; December 13, 1869.

———."Colorado Question Box." October 30, 1955.

———."Contracted Illness in Japan." November 14, 1898.

———."December and May." February 3, 1880.

———."Died." November 5, 1873.

———."Disinherited His Favorite Niece." November 27, 1898.

———."George Beckwith Dead." April 25, 1892.

———."Heavy Real Estate Transactions." March 8, 1885.

———."Mormon Colony." February 28, 1871.

——."Mrs. Elsie Beckwith Dies at Denver Home." August 18, 1931.

——."Rev. L. E. Beckwith." May 12, 1871; May 16, 1871; May 17, 1871; May 21, 1871; May 28, 1871; June 4, 1871.

——."Strayed or Stolen." February 17, 1871.

——."Wife Appointed to Care for Estate of Husband." May 25, 1907.

Rosso, Mike. "The Lariat Loop: An Engineering Marvel at Texas Creek." *Colorado Central Magazine.* July 1, 2016. https://www.coloradocentralmagazine.com/the-lariat-loop-an-engineering-marvel-at-texas-creek/.

Salida Mail. "Still Lives: Canon City Penitentiary Cheated by a Titled Life Convict." August 30, 1892.

Sierra Journal (Rosita, CO). "Personal." November 22, 1883.

Silver Cliff Rustler. May 30, 1900; November 16, 1898; October 5, 1898; September 28, 1904.

"Beckwith Ranch Sold." May 22, 1907.

"Beckwith Ranch Sold Again." October 9, 1907.

"Died." December 30, 1891.

"Hon. E. T. Beckwith." June 12, 1907.

Turk, Gayle. *Wet Mountain Valley: A Quick History.* Colorado Springs: Little London Press.

Vital Records of Norwich 1659–1848, Part 1. Hartford, CT: Hartford Society of Colonial Wars in the State of Connecticut, 1913. https://www.loc.gov/item/13009844/.

Walker, Wildra. "Tales from the Old Times: Bridget's Story." *Wet Mountain Tribune* (Westcliffe, CO). July 30, 2009.

Wet Mountain Tribune (Westcliffe, CO). February 19, 1926; January 21, 1899; March 4, 1921; November 23, 1901.

——."At Rest." June 15, 1907.

——."Back to the Beckwith Ranch: Wife of Former Ranch Manager Recalls Life at the Historic Property in the 1940s." December 13, 2012.

——."Beckwith Pals Continue Pursuit." April, 10, 1997.

——."Beckwith Ranch Gets Substantial State Restoration Grant." January 31, 2002.

——."Beckwith Ranch Proposal Goes to Public Hearing." February 27, 1997.

——."Beckwith Ranch Receives $133,000 Historical Grant." August 28, 2003.

——."Branded in Time." June 26, 2003.

——."Elton Beckwith Dead." June 1, 1907.

——."Friends of Beckwith Work Hard to Curate Ranch." October 8, 2020.

——."Historic Beckwith Ranch May Be Donated for Restoration." December 19, 1996.

——."Notice of Sale of Cattle for Pasturing, Feeding and Agister Charges." October 22, 1920.

——."Pals of Beckwith Ranch Sign Long Term Lease." January 6, 1998.

——."Pals of Beckwith Ranch Tell of Interior Restoration Project." November 25, 2010.

——."Ranch Reaches Milestone." August 20, 1998.

——."Scenic Byways Board Eyes Quarter Million in Funding." July 6, 2000.

——."With $267,000 in Hand: Beckwith Ranch Restoration Project Enters Phase Two." August 29, 2002.

——."Undersized Lot Puts Squelch on Beckwith Ranch Proposal." March 6, 1997.

——."View of the Ranch Home of A. K. Marselus (Formerly the Beckwith Place)." July 19, 1918.

——."Volunteer Workers Spruce Up Historic Beckwith Ranch." July 16, 1998.

Wilson, Merrill Ann. *Restoration Study for Beckwith Ranch (Waverly Ranch)*. SHF 2004-01-048. Denver: Colorado Historical Society, 2006.

Wulsten, Carl. *The Silver Region of the Sierra Mojada (Wet Mountain) and Rosita, Fremont County*, Colorado. Rosita, CO: Bank of Rosita, 1876. https://www.mtgothictomes.com/custer_county.htm.

Archival Materials

Arapahoe County, Colorado. Marriage license no. 22705. September 14, 1898.

Boston Municipal Court. George C. Beckwith naturalization records. April 1844.

California Bureau of Vital Statistics. Death certificate of Elsie Velma Beckwith Lentz. Certificate no. 14395. December 23, 1931.

Colorado Bureau of Vital Statistics. Death certificate of Elsie A. Beckwith. August 17, 1931.

Colorado Division of Vital Statistics. Marriage record report no. 372. August 25, 1875.

Colorado Division of Vital Statistics. Marriage record report no. B-65, P-488. February 2, 1880.

Colorado Historical Society. Beckwith Ranch historical marker. 2002.

Friends of the Beckwith Ranch. *My Home on the Range.* Unpublished manuscript by George William Hendrickson. 1941.

Lake County, Indiana. Marriage license no. 1677. April 8, 1914.

National Archives. Affidavit signed by Edwin F. Beckwith and William H. Phelps. September 3, 1873.

Elton Beckwith's proof of right of preemption. Certificate no. 887. September 3, 1873.

National Register of Historic Places. Beckwith Ranch registration form. April 24, 1998. https://npgallery.nps.gov/GetAsset/a9cad5da-c1ba-4d86-a2d1-7ebfb91e0afc.

US Census Bureau. Census record of George C. Beckwith. Ellsworth, Maine. July 26, 1850.

Census record of George C. Beckwith. Cambridge, Massachusetts. August 10, 1860.

Census record of George C. Beckwith. Denver, Colorado. June 3, 1870.

US Department of State. Passport application of Edwin F. Beckwith. Washington, DC. Application no. 10997. December 15, 1889.

Passport application of Elton T. Beckwith and Elsie Beckwith. New York. Application no. 36228. January 28, 1901.

Historical Consultants

Elizabeth French, longtime Wet Mountain Valley resident, Beckwith historian, former president of Friends of Beckwith Ranch, and renowned portrayer of Mrs. Beckwith

Larry Green, author of "That Is the Week That Was—Infrequent Notes," a periodic email on railroading

Dick Jones, longtime Wet Mountain Valley resident and historian

Bud Piquette, longtime Wet Mountain Valley resident, historian, and collector of artifacts

Gary Ziegler, longtime Wet Mountain Valley resident, archaeologist, and historian

About the Author

Courtney Miller is an award-winning author with a passion for art, archaeology, astronomy, and history. His seven-book *Cherokee Chronicles* series follows the lives of a fictional Cherokee family through ancient times to westward expansion. This series has won acclaim for its excellent research into the Cherokee way of life. His *White Feather Mysteries* feature White Feather, a character from *Cherokee Chronicles*, in a modern rural mountain setting. This series combines humor, intrigue, and twisting plots to produce page-turning stories for a cozy evening.

Miller has been an active member of the Friends of Beckwith Ranch, helping with renovations and repairs. His efforts have been both practical—helping organize fundraisers and leading tours—and research oriented. He and several other ranch researchers have spent years exploring the history of the Beckwith Ranch, researching the lives of the Beckwith men and women who founded the ranch.